RULE AND REIGN YOUR INTERNAL WORLD OVERCOMING TRAUMA

Developmental Emotional Maturity Skills

Book Three

Angie Meadows

Studies based on the NIV or the KJV versions.

A Thousand Tears, LLC
PO BOX 1373
Huntington, WV 25715
enablersjourney@gmail.com
http://enablersjourney.com
http://angiegmeadows.com/
Rock of Recovery podcast
https://admin5.podbean.com/rockofrecovery/settings/feed
Angie G Meadows YouTube
https://www.youtube.com/channel/UC9lo6RVhc1Ieng_fj8LqFPA

Deliver me, O my God, from the hand of the wicked and from the grasp of evil and cruel abuse. Psalm 71:4

Contents

Introduction

Many wounds are harbored in our subconscious thinking. Any new wound that mimics an old wound or trauma gives us an exaggerated emotion and we revert to core destructive emotional patterns. Negative emotions are a typical response to trauma. Many wounds develop in childhood and are left untreated. Betrayal, abandonment, rejection, neglect, abuse, misunderstood, unstable environment, unstable relationships, and sexual abuse are a few deep inner wounds which would create exaggerated emotions and stunt emotional growth. These wounds fester. Feeling unloved creates internal chaos. Children do not have the emotional structure to handle these wounds. This is where unhealthy core patterns develop.

Let us look at one pattern, if I feel rejection, immediately I feel exaggerated intense and unrelenting self-pity because of an original rejection wound. This new wound causes an avalanche of old wounds that will replay repeatedly in my mind or chronically trigger me by minor offenses. When this happens, the original wound has never healed. Anger or anxiety are common core responses to a trauma wound. This is a repetitive fight or flight anxious state which escalates the need to escape. This feeling drives immature action to deflect the internal pain.

Other core emotional patterns may be fear, self-pity, bitterness, grieving, depression, suicidal thinking, or the development of substance use disorder (SUD). Many individuals with substance use disorder (SUD) report they have ALL these wounds and more. Of course, these painful wounds would damage the inner core and program survival responses of heightened emotions. A myriad of dysfunctional coping skills develops to escape this torment. **Substance Use Disorder is often a result of an untreated trauma and habitual immature core thinking patterns.** Mostly, we are unaware of the forces driving our choices. This teaching will help us recognize the reasons behind our behaviors and how to heal from our traumas and retrain our inner core responses to be safe and healthy. We must train our teens and young adults to process and release trauma so their emotional suffering can be alleviated before they land in severe inner core responses that will devastate their lives.

Recognizing our trauma wounds and retraining our core to think and respond differently is essential to grow and mature. **This maturity skill of being responsible to identify and heal our inner wounds will bring lasting peace.**

PRINCIPLES

1. Healing our emotional wounds brings lasting emotional stability.

2. Adversity causes trauma or builds character.

3. Mental Prisons separate us from God and others.

4. God's thoughts are higher than our thoughts.

5. Spiritual growth and maturity are intentional.

6. Whoever or whatever controls your thinking controls you.

7. Good thinking skills lead to good decision-making skills.

8. Maturity goes emotionally above circumstances.

9. A mature mind is quiet and peaceful.

10. A happy heart is my responsibility to cultivate.

11. There is a time to love and a time to hate.

12. Joy gives strength, health, and happiness.

13. Walking in peace is my responsibility.

14. Love is patient. Patience makes others feel loved.

15. Gentleness, goodness and kindness is heavenly wisdom.

16. Meekness is freedom from arrogance or stubbornness.

17. We cannot please God without faith.

18. True freedom is freedom not to sin.

LESSON 1

TRAUMA TRAP

Rescue me from a violent death: spare my precious life from these dogs (emotional torment and abuse). Psalms 22:20 (NLT)

Introduction

Intentional thinking is a small part of the average person's daily cognitive thinking. We may intentionally think about work or a project, but to intentionally think deeply about why we say, do or feel something is a missing emotional development skill in many of us. Instead, when daily life triggers a trauma wound, it is automatically felt as an exaggerated emotion. Even a small insignificant rejection from someone we really do not know could precipitate a quick slide into the dysfunctional inner core responses because of a previous intense trauma wound. **This makes us unable to trust ourselves.** Some of our responses are so quick that there is not even time to think of the trigger that may have caused the old wound to resurface. If this trigger can be identified, we will know what old trauma wound needs worked through and released.

Lesson

When a surge of anxiety, fear, anger or one of our core responses are felt, pause, and recognize what happened to trigger this emotion. Usually this is not a healthy expression of an emotion, but an exaggerated one, it can be an overwhelming and uncontrollable emotion which can lead to impulsive behaviors. After studying Trauma Chart (Figure 1), you may be able to identify a different core response that you express during times of distress.

As you note from this chart, these inner core responses are pre-programmed in the subconscious and are automatic. This can happen with adults or in childhood, during a traumatic event: accident, divorce, abandonment, neglect, domestic violence, toxic relationship, or a sudden and chronic illness, etc. Also, intense emotional trauma experienced by active military service men and women could **imprint trauma**.

> *Lasting peace will need to address the trauma in our past and help us develop a safe inner self.*

This can be done when we slow down enough to discover our emotional wounds, heal, and choose to retrain our subconscious responses.

		Trauma Trap Evaluation		
		Intentional Thinking Minimalized		
		Automatic Subconscious Thinking Exaggerated		
M E N T A L	TRAUMA	INNER CORE RESPONSES	TRAUMA	M I N D
	-Betrayal		-Rejection	N
	-Abandonment	*Anxiety*	-Bully	D
	-Neglect	*Anger*	-Hypocrite	
	-Misunderstood	*Fear*	-Emotionally	C
	-Insecure	*Grieving*	Wounded	O
P R I S O N S	-Unloved	*Self-Pity*	-Physically	N
	-Unwanted	*Loneliness*	Abused	T
		Depression	-Sexually	R
		Suicidal	Violated	O
		Stubbornness		L
		Hopeless		
		=		
		Intense		
		Suffering		
		Severe Trauma Responses Cutting, suicidal thoughts, homicidal rage, confusion, hopelessness, violence alternating with intense pleasure seeking and the development of other behaviors to escape reality like substance use disorder.		

© 2020 Angie G Meadows Figure 1

Exercise

Separate yourself from your past trauma. To begin, use the Trauma Trap Self-Evaluation (Figure 2) to identify your past traumas, inner core responses and severe trauma responses. Use Trauma Trap (Figure 1) as an example to prompt the discovery of your inner wounds. Identify your past or present traumas and inner core responses along with your severe trauma responses.

TRAUMA Imprint Evaluation			
Intentional Thinking Developed			
Subconscious Thinking/Behaviors Observed			
M E N T A L P R I S O N S	Trauma	Inner Core Responses	Trauma	M I N D C O N T R O L
		Intense Suffering		
Severe Trauma Responses			
© 2020 Angie G Meadows Figure 1b			

Application

Think true, noteworthy, and noble thoughts about yourself.

Finally, brothers, whatever is true, whatever is noble, whatever is right, whatever is pure, whatever is lovely, whatever is admirable —if anything is excellent or praiseworthy— think about such things. Philippians 4:8

| *The balance is to not think too highly of yourself.*

For by the grace given me I say to every one of you: Do not think of yourself more highly than you ought, but rather think of yourself with sober judgment, in accordance with the measure of faith God has given you. Romans 12:3

Now it is important to change your story!

> You are not your past.
> You are not your trauma.
> You are not what has been done to you.

Together we are going to learn, grow and understand our worth, value and preciousness before God.

Principle

Healing our emotional wounds brings lasting emotional stability.

Conclusion

For the next several weeks, recognize your trauma and inner core responses. Next, we will explore the mental prisons and mind control traps caused by trauma. Then we will discover Biblical Thinking Principles from God's Word that can foster our emotional maturity.

We are going to reshape a new identity with an entire emotional make-over. Before this series is over, we will be able to pull subconscious reactions into conscious thinking and repattern them. This will nurture deep healing.

As for me, I will behold your face in righteousness: I shall be
satisfied, when I awake, with your likeness. Psalm 17:15

Lord God would you give me the wisdom to understand my fleshly emotions that drive me to destruction. Help me to be intentional with my thinking. Spare me from being controlled by my emotions or the emotions of others. Let me contend for my freedom from anxiety. Let me pursue you until I awake in your likeness. In Jesus Name, Amen.

LESSON 2

EMOTIONAL MATURITY

No, in all these things we are more than conquerors
through him who loved us. Romans 8:37

Introduction

The next several lessons we will learn how to recognize trauma and our trigger responses, mental prisons, mind control, a carnal mind, the mind of Christ, and identify our healthy and unhealthy heart conditions. When we can identify dysfunctional patterns, we can practice healthy patterns through meditating on healthy thoughts. This is a **maturity skill**; it does not come naturally. Today, we are going to continue the recognition of trauma and choose to respond differently. Do not follow stupid thoughts that lead into a pit of depression. Do not follow fickle, unreliable emotions. We want self-control. It is imperative to observe the things that are painful in our life and grow in character through this adversity and embrace the good. It is possible, that we could miss the precious things in life by being absorbed with negativity. Negativity causes suffering. *So, anything that causes emotional suffering needs processed and released.*

Lesson

RECOGNIZE

Identify which negative behaviors from the Trauma Trap you indulge. Know that it is within your power to develop your intentional thinking skills and recognize negative thoughts and behaviors. Start retraining your responses each day. One way to do this is to give yourself permission to *pause* and do it or say it again. For example:

if you feel anger. Stop. Recognize it. Observe it. Journal about it. Change it into something positive. We call this the rewind game. In the 90's, we needed to rewind VHS tapes. Today, let us learn to rewind bad habits and reshape new ones. So much of our behaviors are just bad habits.

Emotional Maturity			
Intentional Thinking Exercised			
Recognize Subconscious Thinking			
M	RELEASE	RETRAIN	REPLACE	P
E	Stop	Inner Core	Humility	
D	Recognize	Responses	Truthfulness	E
I	Observe	Love	Loyalty	
T	Journal	Joy	Kindness	A
A	Rewind	Peace	Courage	C
T	Redo	Patience	Obedience	
I	Release	Gentleness	Respect	E
O	Reach	Faith	Compassion	F
N		Meekness	Generosity	
	*Do the next	Self-control	Contentment	U
	right things!	=	Flexibility	L
		Freedom	Orderliness	
			Attentiveness	
			Steadfast	
			Grateful	
			Enthusiasm	
			Endurance	
			Determination	
			Dependability	

Refuse to circle this mountain.
Refuse trauma, offense, mistake, problem, or another uncertainty. Clean up compulsive obsessive thinking and impulsive responses. **Reach** out for help. **Reshape** your future.

Some of our behaviors have been programmed into our subconscious from childhood when survival was the goal. If this happened to you, I am sorry you suffered abuse. This was wrong and should have never happened. I am sorry you were not nurtured and protected. Let my heart go out and touch yours with love today.

Ask yourself:

- What triggers my negative inner core responses?
- Am I overreacting?
- When did this emotion become so intense in my life?
- Is there an old trauma wound that needs worked through?

RELEASE & REPLACE

Next, I want you to choose to *release* the emotion and replace it with a character quality or the fruit of the Spirit. For example: *Release* anger by pausing as soon as you feel it. Choose compassion for the person who is irritating you. If it is a person hurting you, use your anger in a positive way to choose to develop boundaries, find safety and protect the innocent. If it is an old wound, choose forgiveness and move forward. This takes time. Be gracious and kind with yourself. Forgive yourself for shortcomings quickly.

> *DO NOT hold onto any failure. Get up! Brush the dust (failure) off your feet and do the next right thing.*

- What is your strongest emotion that needs to be released?

Symptoms of Anger	
Mark each on 1–10. 1=little; and 10=indulged very much?	
• Irritation	
• Frustration	
• Aggravation	
• Impatience	
• Bitterness	
• Stubbornness	
• Arrogance	
• Opinionated	
• Bullying	

Mood Tracer			
Bitterness	Anger	Hatred	Compassion
Self-pity	Moodiness	Loneliness	Patience
Grieving	Depression	Suicidal Thinking	Courage
Gluttony	Addiction	Guilt & Shame	Grace & Mercy

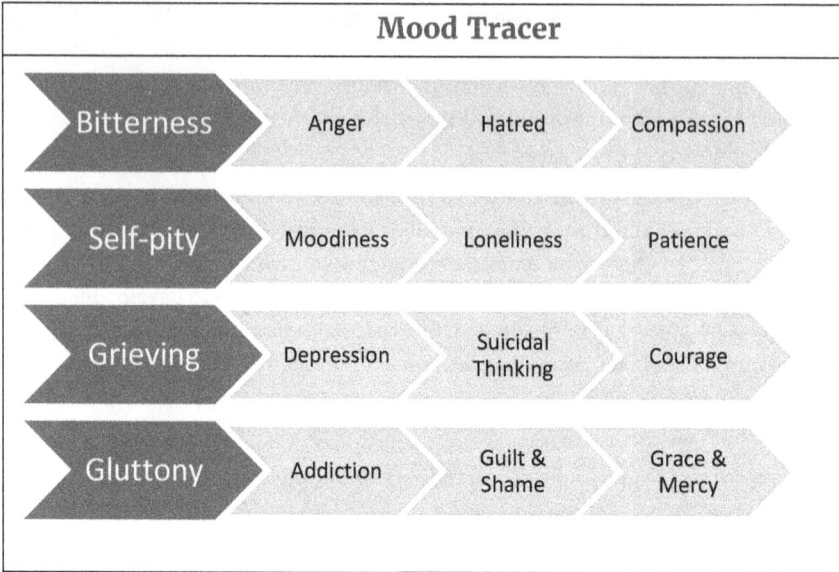

What emotional skill do I need to learn to replace the negative ones? Kindness, compassion, patience, forgiveness, courage, gratefulness, etc.

Do I need to learn to practice grace and mercy? So, name your emotions and then trace how each emotion goes to a stronger more debilitating emotion. Now, instead of indulging and agreeing with a negative emotion, name it, trace where it came from and where it started originally and practice character skills and the fruit of the Spirit.

REFUSE

Emotional Immaturity has passive thinking patterns or ruts formed in your brain. This is where we practice moving from subconscious passive thinking into our conscious awareness of thoughts and feelings. Once you have thought a problem over a few times and there is no resolution, more thinking is not the answer. The answer lies within the power to stop thinking it over and move forward to the next duty, chore, or service on your list for the day.

What situation or circumstance do I repetitively think?

Can I recognize reasoning and rationalizing in my head as a signal that I am heading for trouble? For example: Reasoning: Desperate times means its ok to steal. Rationalizing: Everyone else does it, so it is ok if I do it.

- Is there a person who has too much power over me and dominates my time or my thinking?

- Who are the people who have hurt me that I need to forgive?

RETRAIN

So much of our thinking is immature (dark) and dysfunctional. It takes practice to recognize, release, replace, and refuse to mull over a trauma, offense, mistake, problem, or some other uncertainty. In this stage, you will train yourself what to think and speak. Think of yourself as a mental toddler needing potty training. Toddlers need practice, encouragement, direction, training, patience, and continual coaching over a period of 1-12 months to be fully potty trained. Think of this period in your life as a time for patience with yourself. When you have a diaper moment, do not make a big deal out of it, just clean it up and go on. Apologize without excuses. **Do not carry your dirty diaper. Tomorrow is a new day; begin training again.**

Here is how you apologize without excuse: *I did it and I am sorry.*

Now take a deep breath.
- What emotion is causing great suffering that I need to observe and release?

What fruit of the Spirit do I choose to use to retrain my thinking: Love, joy, peace, patience, gentleness, goodness, faithfulness, meekness, or self-control? I think we may need all of them for some circumstances. Christ chose to not allow evil to dominate or control Him. This is how Jesus did it: *Jesus said, "Father, forgive them, for they do not know what they are doing." Luke 23:34a*

This is the Apostle Paul's solution to evil:
Do not be overcome by evil but overcome evil with good. Romans 12:21
- What good could I do today to overcome the evil that oppresses me?

REACH

When you are stuck, reach out for a trusted friend, sponsor, or counselor. If you keep circling the same mountain and end up with severe trauma responses, you are in a dry and thirsty desert. You are stuck! REACH OUT!

Severe trauma responses: Cutting, suicidal thoughts or suicide attempts, homicidal rage, confusion, hopelessness, violence alternating with intense pleasure thinking and actions to escape reality through mind altering substance use.

- Identify your trusted friend, sponsor, or counselor?
- Who can you go to when you need help to change your thinking?

- Choose several people so you do not wear one of them out.
- Who needs you to befriend or sponsor them?

<u>RESHAPE</u>

If I recognize and clean up my compulsive thinking and my impulsive responses and release, replace, refuse, and retrain them with right thinking and right responses, I can find emotional stability and security and reshape my future. What would it look like to have a life of emotional maturity?

Exercise

Choose one person from the past who has wounded you or from the present that continues to wound you after you forgive them. Forgiveness tears down the dominance and control others have over us, but we must reclaim that ground in our soul and rebuild a defensive fortress strong enough to hold that ground. Now when you are in the presence of a bully who continually stabs you emotionally with nonsense, realize people-pleasing behaviors, fear of others, or need for approval and replace that ground with courage. Courage is strong enough to push back when you are being bullied.

Building A Strong Fortress of Defense		
Immature Behavior of Another	**My Immature Defenses**	**Building my Fortress**
Bully	People pleaser Fear of others Need for approval	Courage
Insensitive	Rejected Wounded Unmet Expectations	Compassion Acceptance
Faintheartedness and relapsing into addiction behaviors	Mental Suffering Emotional Anguish	Grace
Manipulation	Un-forgiveness Bitterness Anger Hatred	Mercy

Application

It is a choice. We are not puppets. We do not have to be pushed into the raging waters of trauma as a victim. We can master our stormy emotions and rise above circumstances and recover from anything. We just need the thinking skills to do this and the confidence to press onward and upward.

Principle

Adversity causes trauma or builds character.

Conclusion

Any anxiety or emotional suffering needs to be pulled from the subconscious into the conscious realm of thinking and analyzed. This thinking skill may require journaling, listening to yourself talk with a friend, or counselor. Find your grumbling and complaining, then you will know what painful memory needs worked through and released. Find your bitterness and you will know who you have not completely forgiven. Forgiveness is not complete if the person is still in your life and continues to wound you with immature behaviors. This necessitates the building of strong fortresses with higher ground of mature character. Now learn to laugh with boldness and confidence when someone tries to assassinate you emotionally. *No, in all these things we are more than conquerors through him who loved us. Romans 8:37*

As for me, I will behold your face in righteousness: I shall be satisfied, when I awake, with your likeness. Psalm 17:15

Lord Almighty God come to me and let me be strong and mighty in spirit. Give me the emotional Skills to build fortresses of courage and boldness. Let compassion, grace and mercy be my friends to honor. When I stumble, let me rise again to brush off disappointments, and failures. Break the strongholds of lies that keep me bound. I am ready, Lord. Make me eager to be in your school of training. Amen

LESSON 3

MENTAL PRISONS

He (God) has sent me to bind up the broken hearted, to proclaim freedom for the captives and release from darkness for the prisoners. Isaiah 61:1b(KJV)

Introduction

Recognize **Mental Prisons** along with the games other people play to control and manipulate. Today, look at your own **self-inflicted prisons.**

Lesson

Mental prisons give an allure of safety, a place of solace and familiar comfort and yet it is a place of deep, dark, and desperate torment.

> *Mental prisons are a place of obsessing, self-defeating emotions, and bondage in negative thinking patterns.*

- Identify Obsessing
- Identify Self-Defeating Emotions
- Identify Signals of Mental Prisons
- Recognize why you are stuck in a Mental Prison.

Exercise

Obsessing	
What type of obsessing plagues you?	
Past wrong done to you	
Past wrongs you have done	
Unchangeable Accidents/Circumstances	
Identifying with Traumas/Wounds	
Indulging negative emotions	
Unhealthy toxic relationship	
Circle any dysfunctional coping skills: Binge watching tv, games, food addictions, lustful thinking, or mood-altering substances.	

Self-Defeating Emotions	
Which ones are inner core response to a wound/trauma?	
• Anxiety, worrying, fretting	
• Anger, bitterness	
• Fear or fear with torment	
• Self-pity, whining, complaining	
• Lonely, withdrawn, avoiding	
• Isolated	
• Grieving, mourning, and sadness	
• Grumpiness, complaining	
• Depression	
• Overwhelming emotions	

Mental Prisons make us emotionally unavailable to others who need us.

Signals of Mental Prisons	
Helpless/Hopeless	
Negative Self-talk	
Automatic Replay traumatic event	

Obsessive thinking	
Impatience or apathetic	
Complacency	
Failure mentality (negative self-talk)	
Victim/Helpless syndrome	
Giving up (faintheartedness)	
Giving in (either to abuse from another or self-destructive behaviors)	
Workaholic (consuming self with busyness)	
Emotionally stuck and unable to move forward	
Discouraged	
Depressed	

Example of mental prison:

Example One: A person who is lonely becomes depressed and isolates and decides to connect with inanimate objects (hoarder); or television shows or actors, musicians, or other emotionally unavailable people.

Example Two: A person who was wounded emotionally in church and vows to never return, carries a grudge, and then allows the wound to harden their heart towards God.

Mental Prisoners cannot get a vision of a different future than the present.

Application

Lord, God in the name of Jesus would You guide me to discover the mental prisons of my thinking.

What is your greatest emotional struggle? Take this struggle to the Lord this week in your journaling. Grieve, forgive, and release. Every time you sense the burden of this prison do it again. Offer this hardship, struggle, wound or trauma to the Lord as your sacrifice. Then flip it and find reasons to be grateful. Make a list of the things you have learned through this difficulty.

Mental Prisons	
Circle the ones that apply and write out any others you identify:	
• Stumbling over another fallen believer	
• Persecution or abuse by believers or unbelievers	
• Sexual violation or abuse	
• Bullies or hypocrites	
• Divorce/betrayal	
• Compulsive self-destructive behaviors	
• Offended against something or someone	
• Domestic violence/child abuse or neglect	
• Severe accident, chronic illness, or war	
• Death of a loved one	
• Addictive thinking or behaviors (yours or someone else's)	
• Financial/job stress	
• Relationship stress	

Principle

Mental Prisons separate us from God and others.

Conclusion

Any emotion not processed is programmed into our subconscious and affects our central nervous system. This can cause a mental prison. When we can identify our trauma wounds and our inner core responses, we can recognize trauma triggers quickly, pull the original trauma into our conscious thinking and process it. Now the healing can begin. Practice repatterning your subconscious thinking as we learned in lesson two.

As for me, I will behold your face in righteousness: I shall be satisfied, when I awake, with your likeness. Psalm 17:15

Lord, God in Jesus name, hear me and heal my soul. Bind up my broken heart and give me freedom. Have mercy on me and set me free from mental prisons. Give me insight and revelation knowledge into the depth of my inner being that I may reclaim all that is rightfully mine. Amen

LESSON 4

IDENTIFYING CARNAL THINKING

Those who live according to the sinful nature have their minds set on what that nature desires; but those who live in accordance with the Spirit have their minds set on what the Spirit desires. Romans 8:5

Introduction

Habitual carnal thinking indulged and nurtured like a pot of homemade stew simmering all day will set the trap for a mental prison. If we ever hope to change, we must recognize the thinking that drives our behaviors. Thirty-five years ago, I declared myself an atheist and embraced carnal thinking. My life was a mess. But take heart, by the grace of God, I found hope!

Lesson

1) **Colossians 2:18** What kind of a mind is identified by false humility, worship of angels, puffed up (arrogant), or idle notions? *Do not let anyone who delights in false humility and the worship of angels disqualify you for the prize, such a person goes into great detail about what he has seen, and his __unspiritual mind__ puffs him up with idle notions.*

2) **Deuteronomy 28:16,28** What happens or should happen if you do not obey and carefully follow the commands of the Lord? *(16) You will be cursed in the*

city and cursed in the country. (28) The Lord will afflict you with madness, blindness, and **_confusion of mind_**.

3) **Deuteronomy 28:65b** What kind of mind is referenced in this verse and what other struggles in verse 64 go along with this type of mind? *(64) Then the Lord will <u>scatter</u> you among all nations, from the end of the earth to the other. There you will <u>worship other gods</u>—gods of wood and stone, which neither you nor your fathers have known. (65b) There the Lord will give you an **anxious mind**, eyes weary with longing, and a <u>despairing heart</u>.*

4) **Job 17:4** What kind of a mind inhibits our triumph? *You have **_closed their minds_** to understanding; therefore, you will not let them triumph.*

5) **Psalm 119:113** What type of mind does the psalmist hate? What does he love? *I hate **_double-minded_** men, but I <u>love your law</u>.* The Merriam-Webster's Dictionary synonym for double-minded is shifty, guile, sneaky, cheating, crooked, deceitful, deceptive, etc.

6) **Proverbs 12:8** What kind of mind is despised? *A man is praised according to his wisdom, but men with **_warped minds_** are despised.*

7) **Proverbs 23:33** What effect does linger long with wine (alcohol) cause your mind to do? *Your eyes will see strange sights and your **_mind imagine confusing things._***

8) **Ezekiel 21:24** If we keep our guilt (iniquity) in our minds by the expression of open rebellion what may happen to us? *"Therefore, this is what the Sovereign Lords says: 'Because you people have **brought to mind your guilt** by your <u>open rebellion</u>, revealing your sins in all that you do—because you have done this, you will be taken <u>captive</u>.'"*

9) **Daniel 4:16** King Nebuchadnezzar had a dream that warned him of judgment because of his pride. He was driven to a field for 7 years until he acknowledged that the Most High God was sovereign over the kingdoms of men. What kind of a mind did God give him? *Let his mind be changed from that of a man and let him be given the **_mind of an animal_**, till seven times pass by for him.*

10) **James 1:6-8** What kind of a mind makes a man unstable? *But when he asks, he **must believe and not doubt**, because he who doubts is like a wave of the sea, blown and tossed by the wind (7) That man should not think he will receive anything from the Lord; (8) he is a **_double-minded man_**, <u>unstable</u> in all he does.*

Exercise

Choose any of the remaining verses and make up your own question and answer study. If you can name a problem, God's Word has an answer with a precept, statute, principle, or command to guide your thinking. Learn to use a Bible Concordance. Do word studies. This skill can unravel any confusion. Make a note of the type of mind you currently indulge. Soon we will claim our inheritance and develop a Christ-like mind. **1 Corinthians 2:16** *...But we have the mind of Christ.*

1) Closed mind Isa. 44:18
2) Deluded mind Jer. 14:14; 23:26
3) Divisive mind with evil thoughts Ezek. 38:10
4) Troubled mind (unable to sleep) Dan. 2:1
5) Terrified mind Dan. 4:5
6) Disturbed mind Dan. 7:15
7) Earthly concerned mind Matt. 16:23
8) "Out of your mind" Acts 12:15
9) Poisoned (evil) mind Acts 14:2
10) Fleshly/Carnal mind Rom. 8:5
11) Fleshly (sinful) mind Rom. 8:7
12) Naïve mind; easily deceived Rom. 16:18
13) Dull, veiled (blinded) mind 2 Cor. 3:14
14) Blinded mind by the god of this age 2 Cor. 4:4
15) Deceived mind; led astray 2 Cor. 11:3
16) Minding earthly things brings shame Phil. 3:19
17) Corrupt minds robbed of the truth 1 Tim. 6:5
18) Depraved minds oppose the truth 2 Tim. 3:8
19) Unbelievers have corrupted minds and consciences Tit. 1:15

Application

Our own thoughts bind us in mental prisons. I do not have the luxury of thinking my own thoughts. They are anxious, fearful, bitter, self-absorbed, etc. If I identify my carnal thinking and reject it and develop the mind of Christ, I can walk in a place of total peace. *Trust in the Lord with all your heart and lean not on your own understanding; in all your ways acknowledge him, and he will make your paths straight. Proverbs 3:5-6*

Principle

God's thoughts are higher than our thoughts.

Conclusion

The only way to battle the enemy of confusion or double mindedness is to ask for wisdom from God. Search God's Word for wisdom and apply it to your life. *If any of you lacks wisdom, he should ask God, who gives generously to all without finding fault, and it will be given to him. James 1:5*

As for me, I will behold your face in righteousness: I shall be satisfied, when I awake, with your likeness. Psalm 17:15

Lord Jesus, deliver me from my double-minded confusion, help me to seek and search your Word for wisdom like I am searching for hidden treasure. Help me to find the Words of life and eat them. Nourish me to become Mighty in Spirit. (James 1:6-8; Proverbs 2:4; Jeremiah 15:16; Zechariah 4:6.)

LESSON 5

RECOVERY FROM A MENTAL PRISON

... for "Who has known the mind of the Lord so as to instruct him?" But we have the mind of Christ. 1 Corinthians 2:16

Introduction

Your emotions are fickle and cannot be trusted. Whenever your peace is gone, if you do not slow down and process what robbed your peace, you are on the way to an emotional (carnal) thinking pattern and a mental prison.

Now in recovery you need to develop gateways to protect your soul. Your eyes, ears, mind, heart are the main gateways. It takes intentional disciplining our lives through the power of the Holy Spirit to protect these gates.

- Spiritual eyes
- Spiritual ears
- Heart of Christ
- Mind of Christ

And you must find Calvary. Calvary is a place where we learn to suffer well.

Lesson

Spiritual Eyes

As you draw close to God your spiritual eyes will be enlightened and you will have hope and see the glorious riches of your inheritance. *Ephesians 1:18*

Where there is no vision (revelation), the people perish (cast off restraint): but he that keeps the law (hold God's Word esteemed and revered), happy is he. Proverbs 29:18 KJV

Well, my friends, we must have a vision for our future of peace in Christ. Without this revelation of why we exist, there will be no reason for us to restrain the carnal side of our self and nurture the spiritual side. The eyes are a gateway to our minds. We must be vigilant about what we will and will not allow our eyes to gaze upon. Job made a covenant with his eyes to not look lustfully upon a maiden. *Job 31:1*

Spiritual Ears

When we accept a wound (offense), we lose our peace and begin to stumble.

But since they have no root, they last only a short time. When trouble (affliction) or persecution comes because of the Word, they quickly fall away (have no root). Mark 4:17

When we forget the provisions of the Lord and His promises. Our perception is skewed, and our understanding is faulty.

Do you have eyes but fail to see, and ears but fail to hear? And don't you remember? Mark 8:18

Be careful what you allow your ears to hear.

Allow no obscenity or foolish talk or coarse joking. Ephesians 5:4

Let no one deceive you with empty words. Ephesians 5:6

Heart of Christ

Forgetfulness of God's provisions will lead to a hardened heart *(Mark 8:17)* A stubborn refusal to believe and the deceitfulness of sin also hardens the heart. It could be your sin or the sin of another. *(Hebrews 3:12-13) (Mark 16:14)*

Now, *"...that Christ may dwell in your hearts by faith; that you, being rooted and grounded in love... may be able to comprehend... and to know the love of Christ... and may be filled with the fulness of God. (Ephesians 3:17-19)*

Next, we will do a heart study, and you will be able to evaluate the condition of your heart and lay it open before God as the psalmist David. David asked God to enlarge his heart (KJV) or set it free (NIV). *I run in the path of your commands, for you have set my heart free (enlarged my heart). Psalm 119:32*

For now, *above all else, guard your heart. Proverbs 4:23* Make others earn the right to become a close and trusted friend.

Mind of Christ

The natural man cannot receive the things of God; they are foolishness unto him... because they are spiritually discerned... But we have the mind of Christ. *(1 Corinthians 2:14,16)* Mentally we must "be still" and know that God is in control and give Him room in our hearts to teach us to trust Him. (Psalm 46:10)

Busy minds can lead to creativity and joyful industriousness or to torment. Be careful what you allow yourself to dwell on. *For as a man thinks in his heart, so is he. Proverbs 23:7 (KJV)*

<u>Find Calvary</u>

I am crucified with Christ and I no longer live, but Christ lives in me. The life I live in the body, I live by faith in the Son of God, who loved me and gave himself for me. Galatians 2:20

My independence in myself is death. Dependency upon God is strength and not weakness.

A **weak will** cannot say no to myself.

I need to develop a **spiritually strong will**... strong enough to submit to the divinity of God. Strong enough to stop any negative thought patterns or behaviors and control anything I think, say, or do.

A **strong will** needs to be yielded to God for Him to divinely impart His presence to us so we can stop fretting thoughts and replace them with the truth of God's promises. There is a time to learn to suffer well.

Exercise

Seeing and hearing spiritually? Or are you blind and deaf?

Discerning my Spiritual Condition	
1. Have I placed a protective boundary around my eyes, ears, mind, and heart?	
2. Can I hear the truth in Scripture?	
3. Is Scripture alive to me?	
4. Do I seek out instructions in Scripture for my life?	
5. Can I recognize when the Lord is speaking to me?	
6. Can I look at an uncontrollable circumstance in my life and trust the Lord?	
7. Is my heart free enough to follow Christ, no matter what?	
8. Can I say no to myself?	

Application

An awareness of my spiritual side can be a foreign concept. Recognizing my weakness and seeking to develop the heart and mind of Christ is a journey to wholeness. This is a life-long process of growing maturity. The rewards are righteousness, joy and peace and all good things. Let your heart long for the true riches of the kingdom of God. *For the kingdom of God is not a matter of eating and drinking, but of righteousness, peace, and joy in the Holy Spirit. Romans 14:17*

Principle

Spiritual growth and maturity are intentional.

Conclusion

The difference between mental prisons and mind control is that I place myself in a mental prison because of past traumas and my inner core responses to negative events in my life. With mind control, someone else exerts dominance over me and controls my thinking and actions and has taken me captive. We are more vulnerable to mind control if we are experiencing our own mental prison traps of thinking. This lesson is teaching us to guard the gateways to our soul: eyes, ears, mind, and heart. Healing comes when we fix our eyes on Christ and not on things of this world. *He shall not be afraid of evil tidings: his heart is fixed, trusting in the Lord. Psalm 112:7KJV*

As for me, I will behold your face in righteousness: I shall be satisfied, when I awake, with your likeness. Psalm 17:15

Oh Lord God, I am bound in torment of emotions, and I need You. Please teach me how to have the mind of Christ. Help me to fix my mind upon you and believe Your promises. Amen.

LESSON 6

MIND CONTROL

A prudent man sees danger and takes refuge, but the simple keep going and suffer for it. Proverbs 22:3

Introduction

Mind Control is defined as causing changes to the mind or to behavior of another through persuasion and influence. There are ethical and **respectful influences** that respect the individual's personality and rights. Then there are negative influences that strip the person of his/her right to independent thinking.

> **Selfishness** is one of the key components of a person exercising mind control over another.

Lesson

Mind Control manipulators have an agenda. There are numerous mind control tactics used by television, politicians, friends, teachers, coaches, pastors, etc. Most people do not even recognize when they are thinking thoughts placed in their minds by others. This injecting of ideas and beliefs into another is how cults control people or how an abuser keeps his victim captive. Mind Controllers train the subconscious mind of another in the way they want them to think.

Why is mind control used?

- Fulfill another person's agenda
- Defraud you of your money
- Control your time

The End Results of Mind Control

- The victim believes the messages given to them.
- They may even believe so strongly that they can convince another of their new ideas.
- Frequently, loved ones do not recognize them (Personality changes).
- They are given a pseudo-personality: this personality agrees with their abuser/ manipulator's values, beliefs, and ideas (Stockholm syndrome).
- Often this dominance is associated with sexual abuse.

Mind Control Techniques

1) Fear is used for emotional control.

2) Shower of love and affection (aka "love bombing")

3) Loyalty to a destructive person (aka "trauma bonding").

4) Your time is heavily consumed. Individuality is not respected.

5) Increasingly loud repetition of the same words is common.

6) Creating dependency (especially with finances) and controlling your income

7) Verbal abuse, criticism, and insults

8) Threats and bullying

9) Small rewards for desired behavior (aka "bone throwing")

10) Punishment for unwanted behavior (This could be 5 hours to 5 days of ranting to build a case to justify your next physical beating.)

11) Victims are ignorant of the cycle and do not recognize the next phase coming.

12) Victims are often trapped and become unwilling participants. Children are often caught in this cycle.
13) Guilt and shame and bringing up past offenses are used often to dominate and control.
14) You are expected to denounce healthy friends and family.
15) Abuser rails and berates anyone who could protect you until they make you think others are the true enemy.
16) Your loyalty is the only thing that gives you temporary relief.
17) You are made to believe you are making your own decisions.
18) Other manipulation tactics are avoidance, silent treatment, withdrawing their heart from you, lying and hiding.
19) This abuse is always accompanied by financial dominance.

Next Stage of Mind Control
1) Guilt is established, and the victim feels like they deserve the punishment.
2) The abuser's ability to unrealistically rationalize the injustices done to them is established.
3) The assault on your identity continues and everything you say is contradicted.
4) Your individuality is rejected.
5) Who you are is redefined. Your identity as an individual person is being eroded.
6) Any movement towards freedom reverts the abuser into a master victim role.
7) They quickly triangulate family and friends by distorting the facts and using emotions to gather support.

Advanced Stage of Mind Control
• When you have completely **lost your identity** and are totally under their control is the only time there is a moment of harmony.
• The abuse will stop momentarily, before it cycles again. This is what I call keeping you on the hook.
• Your new identity becomes apparent.
• You can no longer think your own thoughts.
• Your concerns are for the other person and not yourself.
• You doubt your capability of decision making because all your decisions are met with a massive amount of confusion.
• You are told you are crazy and no longer possess the power to make your own decisions. Even if you do make decisions, none of your boundaries are respected.

Master Mind Controller
• Spends days, weeks, months and even years separating you from anyone safe.
• You feel no one loves you except your manipulator.
• You willingly give them everything.
• You become their "savior" or rescuer.
• Appearances to the outside world can be all good and happy. Skeletons are safely tucked in the closet.
• When you start fighting for your freedom, everything will escalate, and the craziness will be apparent to all.

Exercise

Evaluate your current relationships: marriage, children, employer, etc. Examine any dysfunction in your life. Focus on the good. Establish some future goals for improvement within your control. Empower yourself to become independent. **Now, reshape your future to look different from your past.**

Application

If you have been dominated mentally with mind control games, you are not free to have your own feelings or think your own thoughts. You may be completely unable to make decisions based upon what is best for you. Frequently, you make decisions and get confused or cannot follow through with them. Being dominated with mind control keeps you from feeling like you can trust yourself. If you can recognize this unhealthy relationship, turn to a trusted friend, counselor, or domestic violence shelter to receive help and this will break the cycle. Expect to have a mental and emotional fight to reclaim your life. Distance is needed for your safety. You may also need legal counsel for protective orders to be set in place.

> *Freedom will come when you yield to respectable counsel and not confused emotions.*

Principle

Whoever or whatever controls your thinking, controls you.

Caution

If you escape a toxic relationship and do not do the work to change your thinking and recognize this type of dominance and abuse, you are likely to repeat this scenario the rest of your life. For example: If you spent your teen years fighting back to get free from toxic authorities and did not do the work to build strong foundational thinking, you have likely become trapped in other toxic relationships. You may have even learned to equate mind control dominance with love and perpetuated the cycle of toxicity. This can never bring about strong, healthy relationships.

Until we can evaluate our losses and gains, we cannot understand where we have been, and the work needed to move forward. Today identify what trauma needs healed. If there is time, break out into small group and share with one another your greatest wound.

Wound Identifier
What were the circumstances from childhood or early adulthood that could be the root causes for addictive behaviors and/or dysfunctional coping skills?
I would like for you to name all the destructive influences of your childhood. Add any other circumstances not listed that may have caused you a wound.

Identify Childhood Set Up (Mark yes/no)	
Domestic Violence	
Abandoned	
Neglected	
Brain Washed with mind control	
Incest/Rape	
Enabling parent	
Verbally abusive parent/sibling	
Alcoholic in the home	
Substance use disorder	
Severe street drug use	
Homelessness	
Divorce	
Unable to please parents	
Not validated	
Not safe	
Unable to feel comforted/loved	
Promiscuous parent	
Parental marital conflict	
Single Parent	
No parent	
Emotionally absent parent	
Incarcerated parent	
Abusive siblings	
Bullying peers	
Given drugs or alcohol at a young age	
Other:	

2) What are the outcomes from your emotional childhood pain?
It is important to understand the consequences of this negativity.
Add any insight to your list.

Outcome:	
Confusion	
Fear	
Anxiety	
Stubbornness	

Rebellion	
Misplaced values	
Poor decision maker	
Habitual liar	
Negative thinking or racing thoughts	
Exaggerated emotions	
Unforgiving/bitter	
Irresponsible	
Mental Confusion	
Mental Torment	
Fantasy escape (addictive thinking)	
Depression	
Enabler (over responsible)	
No moral compass	
Passive/aggressive behaviors	
Addictive behaviors (This could be as simple as food compulsions.)	
Self-mutilation (cutting)	
Self-destructive (alcohol/drugs/excessive gambling, pronography)	
Promiscuity	
High-risk behaviors	
Other:	

3) What good things did you have as a child?

Let us make a positive shift and find the good things and develop an attitude of gratitude.

Childhood Comforts:	
Nice Friend	
Friendly personality	
Pets that I loved	
I wanted to do right	
Intelligent	
Good with my hands/crafty	
Hobbies	
Athletic	
Musically inclined	
Loving grandparent	

Stable adult influence	
Food	
Shelter	
Home	
Kind teacher	
Other:	
4) Who did you identify most with as a child? It is good to evaluate the people you admired. They have helped you build your identity. For example, have you practiced dysfunctional behaviors like one of your parents? This may have been an attempt to identify with them to win their approval.	
Peers	
Absent Parent or abusive/enabling parent	
Older sibling	
Sports hero	
Historical hero	
Cult/gang leader	
Musician	
Do you identify with healthy or unhealthy individuals?	
Did you identify with those you were trying to please?	
Did you identify with one who was emotionally unavailable?	
Did you lead or follow a crowd?	

Conclusion

No one deserves the right to usurp your ability to think for yourself. Thinking a thought all the way through to the end is work. Pondering decisions through to their potential or expected outcomes is a learned skill. It is vital to learn God's Word. The commandments reveal to us who/what to obey. The statutes are God's value system. Principles in God's Word helps us establish boundaries. Precepts is a general rule of action. It teaches us how to think for ourselves. Until we can identify the mind control of the media or other influences in our lives, we cannot break its power over us. Purpose to think great thoughts. Thoughts that are higher than yourself. Know the mind of Christ is available for you.

For who has known the mind of the Lord that he may instruct him?
But we have the mind of Christ. 1 Corinthians 2:16

Oh God, dispel the darkness. Show me the lies I believe. Give me courage to fight for my freedom. Help me to build my thinking in the foundational truths of the Word of God. Empower me in Christ to make right decisions. Amen

LESSON 7

RECOVERY FROM MIND CONTROL

For as he thinks in his heart, so is he. Proverbs 23:7

Introduction

Developing decision-making skills empowers us to escape the mind control trap. We are continually being bombarded with false ideology to fulfill the agenda of others.

There are many decisions we make for the benefit of others that we love and cherish. We sacrifice our needs to serve our families. This is the solid ground of loving families, neighbors, and work environments. This is hard to do if we have not been nurtured nor have a healthy identity; instead, we may make rash decisions out of stubbornness or another dysfunctional inner core response. Pause and evaluate options. Take time for yourself, time to reflect, time to pray and time to receive sound counsel. This is not selfish; this is responsible self-care.

Lesson

Identify when you make an impulsive or rash decision to escape dominance or other toxicity. If you resent or regret your recent decisions, it may be because you were manipulated by someone else's belief or agenda. If you made a life altering decision quickly like quitting a job or walking away from stability you were probably triggered by a trauma wound and fleeing quickly was an impulse decision without thought.

It is possible that you are unable to make good decisions because you no longer know how to think your own thoughts. Learn to make decisions slowly (unless you are in danger). Many will **not** decide because they have no good choices or do not know the next step. You do not have to know the next step. Nor does the decision need to be permanent. It needs to be a decision for safety and stability. Ask for counsel from trusted friends and family. Do not let yourself be coerced or abused. Dominance and control from selfish people can cause you to react and not intentionally think through decisions. This will never end well!

| *Impulsive decisions rarely turn out well.*

Decision Making
How to nurture a sanctified self (not a selfish self):
1) If you are empty, take the time to nurture yourself by exercising your internal voice to speak kindness and peace to yourself.
2) It is the principle of placing the oxygen mask on yourself if an airplane decompresses or you will not be able to help anyone else.
3) It is not selfish to exercise your NO muscle if your plate is full of other commitments.
4) Do not ever say YES to a manipulator or abuser unless you need to do this to secure safety for you and your children until you can find a way of permanent escape.

Place your Family First
1) If there are innocent ones under your authority being abused, i.e., children, elderly or handicapped, you must learn be a protector.
2) Balance taking care of yourself and taking care of others is vital to a healthy environment.
3) This care does not apply to the manipulative, abusive, addicted or dominating family members, unless you have the mental and emotional stability and the social support to do so. It would be optimal to do this by moving in and out of these relationships quickly and becoming more and more independent from their control and able to make decisions based upon what is good long-term.

4) Make decisions slowly and think through your decisions and the potential future outcomes.

Make your own Decisions

1) While maturing, we must submit to others. *(Ephesians 5:21)* The reason we do this is because we cannot trust ourselves to make good decisions. But quickly learn to take a thought and think it through to the end.
Do not let toxic people think for you or place yourself under weak leadership.

2) When we are out of control or self-destructive, we must yield and let others who can be trusted to guide us.
Do not let toxic thinking run your life.

3) Work with a trusted friend, teacher or counselor and develop short- and long-term goals and make decisions based upon your goals and not on your emotions.

More Difficult Decisions

1) What is your short-term goal?

2) What are your options?

3) Collect information on each option.

4) Outline choices with possible outcome scenarios.

5) Choose an option. Pray about this decision.

6) Act

Still Struggling
1) State the problem.
2) Pray and ask God for wisdom, a good friend or counselor.
3) Seek God's principles on a related scenario in Scripture. What would Jesus do?
4) State your outcome goals.
5) What do you need to empower yourself to be able to make healthier decisions?

Do not give your decision-making power away. If you have done so and are in an unsafe relationship, work to empower yourself. This may mean you need to educate yourself and to develop job skills and make yourself employable. Work on your freedom from any toxic behaviors, toxic emotional patterns of thought or toxic relationships. This means you must learn to submit to authority even if they are not perfect and still dealing with their own junk.

Indulging toxic emotions rob us, leave us empty and make us vulnerable to be abused, neglected, and abandoned.

> **Name your addictive (toxic) relationships.** You will know they are addictive because they make you emotionally unstable.

Toxic Thinking Traps keep me from making decisions and enjoying my day. When I recognize one of these dysfunctional thinking patterns, a dysfunctional decision is around the corner.

Toxic Thinking Traps
1) Rationalizing
2) Reasoning
3) Obsessing over a person or situation
4) Self- Pity
5) Brooding and moody
6) Angry or bitter
7) Fearful or anxious
8) Sulking and embracing melancholy
9) Lack of joy in the present moment
10) Having to know future outcomes
11) Needing to see the big picture and certain success before moving forward.
12) Fairytale perfectionist daydreaming

Poor Options
1) Sometimes the lack of good options keeps you from making decisions.
2) Yucky option #1
3) Yuckier option #2
4) Choose the least yucky option.
5) It is not possible to know the future, but do not let that keep you stuck.

6) You may need to make hard decisions to make your future look different from your past.

More Suggestions

1) Seek counsel from others who know and love you and will counsel you with the truth but are **willing to let you make your own decision.**

2) Grab a friend to talk things over. Frequently, I say my own answer as I am talking without even knowing that I know the answer.

3) Do not talk yourself into or out of anything.

4) Good decisions feel right and safe.

5) Strong emotional support will empower and undergird you with the strength and support to correct your wrong thinking.

6) You need a professional counselor if you had childhood emotional, physical, or sexual abuse, are in domestic violence or emotionally triggered often. If not, uncontrollable self-destruction behaviors are near.

7) Look at the whole picture past, present, and future.

8) Be aware of your emotions, internal conflicts, lies or negative and defeating thoughts.

9) Make decisions based upon facts, not emotions.

During a Crisis

1) Think temporary decisions

2) Quick temporary decisions may be more manageable until you have time to plan.

3) Deal with your exaggerated emotions before deciding.

4) Make permanent decisions when you do not feel pressured.

5) If you procrastinate, decisions will be made for you by others or the situation may be worsen.

Past Decisions: Good and Bad

1) What were your internal feelings?
(Think about your last major decision.)

2) What were your hesitations?

3) Did you have doubts?
4) Did it work out?
5) What would you do the same?
6) What would you do differently?
7) If you are warm, fed and dry and not being abused, the best decision is to stay and work through your anxiety, anger, or any other exaggerated emotion. Do not run! Instead, take a time out and learn ways to discharge highly exaggerated emotions.

Principle

Good thinking skills lead to good decision-making skills.

Application

Complaints: Listen to your complaints. They are a signal of something you need to be actively discussing with a trusted mentor. Stop looking at others and look at what you need to correct in yourself. *You hypocrite, first take the plank out of your own eye, and then you will see clearly to remove the speck from your brother's eye. Matthew 7:5*

Conclusion

It is not easy to break the power of mind control. The best way I have found is to **distance myself** from abusers and surround myself with healthier people. Also, developing a nurturing parent role and re-parenting myself with protection can be within my power. Just this one behavior may make me bold enough to push back and protect myself from false ideology and confusion. Find a safe space to think your own thoughts and to heal. Speaking hopeful, healing thoughts to yourself is powerful enough to overcome any negative thinking traps.

For as he thinks in his heart, so is he. Proverbs 23:7

Lord help me clean up my impulsive negative thinking. Help me reign in my passive thoughts and rule and reign in the space between my ears. Let no past failure hold me back. Let me progressively move forward to claim all you want me to enjoy! Amen

LESSON 8

SOBER THINKING PRINCIPLES

Have no fear of sudden disaster...Proverbs 3:25

Introduction

Foundational Scriptural principles instruct us to take charge of our thinking. **We cannot let emotions rule our decisions.** There must be solid ground to mature thinking.

Lesson

THINK MATURELY
1) **Think and speak in terms of maturity**

Identifying our thinking and inner core emotions is key to challenging their validity. Many thoughts and emotions have been birthed out of lies. Speak to yourselves in a healthy manner. If we want to be whole, we cannot keep predicting disaster.

For as he thinks in his heart, so is he...Proverbs 23:7 (KJV)

What does your self-talk say to you?

My negative self-talk and obsessing stopped when I learned to speak kindly to myself. Intentionally turn off the negative and preach the promises of God and renounce the dooms day cloud.

2) Regeneration and Renewal leads to Restoration

There is a process of receiving God's mercy and cooperating with the Holy Spirit to heal us from the inside out. This inner washing (forgiving and repenting) and having the power to change comes from asking for God's mercy.

(3) At one time we too were foolish, disobedient, deceived and enslaved by all kinds of passions and pleasures. We lived in malice and envy, being hated, and hating one another. (5) (He saved us...) Not by works of righteousness which we have done, but according to his mercy he saved us, by the washing of regeneration, and renewing of the Holy Ghost; Titus 3:3,5(KJV)

What dysfunctional behaviors or exaggerated emotions stole my freedom today?

3) Honorable living produces teachability

There are two-character traits in this verse: moral purity and humility. *Discipline yourself* to **not** look at moral filth and evil. Instead, *be humble* and focus on the truth of God's Word.

Therefore, get rid of all moral filth and evil that is so prevalent and humbly accept the word planted (engrafted) in you, which can save you. James 1:21

What do I need to do to be humble before God and others?

Lust and anger are siblings. To defeat lust, you must address your anger. Anger is rooted in unforgiveness and pride or some other deep wound to protect yourself.

4) **Discipline your thinking to stop dwelling on things that are not happening.**

Often the hardest maturity skills to learn is to not think every stupid thought that comes into our head. **Recognize the thought and observe it, but do not identify with it.** Once you have thought on something and it cannot be fixed or changed today, then stop thinking about it and go and enjoy your day.

(4) The weapons we fight with are not the weapons of the world. On the contrary, they have divine power to demolish strongholds. (5) We demolish arguments (imaginations) and every pretension that sets itself up against the knowledge of God, and we take captive every thought to make it obedient to Christ. 2 Corinthians 10:4-5

What thoughts cause me suffering and need changed?

5) **Press into God's Word until it comes alive and active in your Spirit.**

Many years ago, I dutifully read my Bible every day. When I shut the book, I had no clue what I had read. So, I challenged God and said, "if this is your Word, you make it alive in me. If not, it is just words on a page." Within hours my friend gave me an easier version of the Bible to read, and it read like a story. I finish the entire Bible within a few weeks. The Word was alive!

For the word of God is living and active. Sharper than any double-edged sword, it penetrates even to dividing soul and spirit, joints, and marrow; it judges the thoughts and attitudes of the heart. Hebrews 4:12

Find a verse to replace your toxic thinking. If that seems impossible go to Hebrews 12; Psalm 103; James 3; or John 15.

6) **Our responsibility is to renew our minds, not to let emotions make us unstable and driven by the wind.**

One of the greatest blessings of finding Christ, is finding peace from a tormented mind. I do not know how to comprehend eternal salvation, but a quiet, peaceful heart and mind is a priceless gift of following the Savior.

Do not conform any longer to the pattern of this world but be transformed by the renewing of your mind. Then you will be able to test and approve what God's will is—his good, pleasing, and perfect will.

Name one way to stop conforming to the world.

Name one way to intentionally transform and renew your mind.

(5) If any of you lacks wisdom, he should ask God... (6) But when he asks, he must believe and not doubt, because he who doubts is like a wave of the sea, blown and tossed by the wind. (7) That man should not think he will receive anything from the Lord; (8) he is double-minded man, unstable in all he does. James 1:5-8

Name one thing that causes you doublemindedness.

❙ *Doublemindedness is a constant mental storm.*

7) **God does His part, and we are responsible to cooperate and do our portion.**

This is work. Working out our salvation is being consciously aware of an imbalance in our lives and asking God to give us wisdom for healing.

(12) ...continue to work out your salvation with fear and trembling, (13) for it is God who works in you to will and to act according to his good purpose. Philippians 2:12b-13

What do I struggle with the most that I need to completely turn over to the Lord? When I am striving, I am doing my own will. When I am emotionally resting, I will be capable of doing God's will. Now, name your struggles and give them to the

Lord.

Emotionally

Physically

Financially

Relationally

8) **A consistent and intentional act of choosing the fruit of the Spirit as an inner core response will heal a trauma wound. A whole person does not have a need to act with a selfish nature.**

> *Could a selfish nature be a protective mechanism to keep our hearts from suffering and hide our emotional wounds?*

Exercise

The acts of the selfish nature become habitual. The wounded spirit opens us up to inner core responses that cause deep suffering and in general, it seems we default to these dysfunctional coping skills to give momentary release of emotional pain or to feel like we are in control. Even though, these behaviors cause more wounds and more trauma. They, also, give us drunk/inebriated relationships that are characterized by intense passion and intense confusion. We need a safe place to heal.

(19) The acts of the sinful nature are obvious: sexual immorality, impurity, and debauchery; (20) idolatry and witchcraft: hatred, discord, jealousy, fits of rage selfish ambition, dissensions, factions (21) and envy; drunkenness, orgies, and the like...Galatians 5:19-21

(22) But the fruit of the Spirit is love, joy, peace, patience, kindness, goodness, faithfulness, (23) gentleness and self-control... Galatians 5:22-23

What relationships are selfish and not sober? Who are your safe people?

When we heal from trauma and change our inner core responses to the fruit of the Spirit **selfishness will disappear.**

> *Selfishness is clinging to the flesh and trying to do the work that only the Holy Spirit can do.*

Name what/who is causing you suffering? Is there anything within your power to change?

Application

Be completely changed. This *renewed thinking* takes time and a consistent intentional choosing of <u>mature</u> character. Be gracious and show yourself kindness as you are growing and maturing.

Therefore, if anyone is in Christ, he is a new creation; the old has gone, the new has come! 2 Corinthians 5:17

What old nature do you need to renounce and fight against?

I renounce _____in the name of Jesus Christ.

I will intentionally fight against _____.

Principle

Maturity goes emotionally above circumstances.

Conclusion

The prophet Habakkuk is describing his mature response to tragedy. There are no figs, no grapes, no olives, no food in the fields, no sheep, and no cattle. And yet, he <u>chooses to rejoice</u> in the Lord. The Lord gives him strength to have feet like a deer. A deer is very steady on the rocks, cliffs, and ledges of a mountain. This is an analogy of higher ground... above circumstances and certainly above the prophet's fears (pounding heart, quivering lips, achy bones and shaky legs).

(16) I heard and my heart pounded, my lips quivered at the sound; decay crept into my bones and my legs trembled. Yet I will **wait patiently** for the day of calamity to come on the nation invading us. (17) Though the fig tree does not bud and there are no grapes on the vines, though the olive crop fails, and the fields produce no food, though there are no sheep in the pen and no cattle in the stalls, (18) yet I will **rejoice** in the LORD, I will be **joyful** in God my Savior. (19) The Sovereign **LORD is my strength; he makes my feet like the feet of a deer; he enables me to go on the heights (mine high places).** Habakkuk 3:16-19

You may have to review the Trauma Trap Chart in Lesson One.

Higher Ground Emotional Trainer
1) Recognize the thought or action that triggered the trauma anxiety.
2)Recognize the preprogrammed inner core response. Were you able to recognize your imbalance immediately or did it simmer and slowly get you out of balance over several days?
3) Take one uncontrollable circumstance in your life and go above the negative emotions and be joyful in God. This is a conscience choice. You can choose how you feel.
4) Its most likely not about you. Do not take things personal. Develop broad

shoulders and thick skin.

Exercise: Slow down and take a deep breath and rebalance. A long slow 4 seconds inhale and 6-7 second exhale will disengage the fight or flight sympathetic nervous system and the exaggerated emotional response and engage your calm parasympathetic nervous system.

5) If it was about you, repent quickly or forgive and release yourself and/or the other person.

6) Now **choose** a fruit of the Spirit response: love, joy, peace, patience, kindness, goodness, faithfulness, gentleness, and self-control.

For example: If you feel rejection, you can choose patience and love for the person and then trust that they can find their own way in life without interference from you.

7) Consider this a test of character. Choose a character skill to work on.

These healthy character choices will give stability and heal trauma and reprogram inner core responses.

Circle the trait you want to work on today.

      Character: humility, truthfulness, loyalty, kindness, courage, obedience, respect, compassion, generosity, contentment, flexibility, orderliness, attentiveness, steadfast, gratefulness, enthusiasm, endurance, determination, and dependability.

8) When a negative emotion comes, you have about 3-5 seconds to reject it before it takes hold in your mind and forces itself to be played out.

Listen to and acknowledge any grumbling and complaining. Grumbling and complaining are good indicators that you are out of balance and have work that needs done to recalibrate and find your peace. Grumbling, complaining, or bitterness are a quick road back to TRAUMA thinking.

If the work is not done soon, suffocating anxiety may develop. It is necessary to discover the emotional responses to a wound that leads to the addiction of negative thinking traps. Brain chemicals produced by indulging negative emotions can be addictive and become dysfunctional friends.

> But I tell you that men will have to give account on the day
> of judgment for every careless word they have spoken. For by your
> words, you will be acquitted, and by your words you will be
> condemned. Matthew 12:36-37

Lord break the chains of passive (drunken) thinking. Let me discover the things that bind me repeatedly. I am tired of grinding the grain of anxiety. Release me and empower me to heal. In your mighty name I pray. Amen.

LESSON 9

MIND OF CHRIST

Set your mind on things above, not on earthly things.
Colossians 3:2

Introduction

<u>Self-regulation is a maturity skill</u>. This simple question evaluation will help determine how much work needs done to calm your thinking. The only way I can regulate my thoughts is to stop thinking my own thoughts and think God's thoughts. His thoughts are based on truth. My thoughts are based on insecurities, trauma wounds, and outright lies. My mind will heal when I regulate my thoughts to come in line with true, honest, just, pure, lovely, and thoughts of good report, virtuous, and praiseworthy. (Philippians 4:8) Learn to kick out thoughts that cause anxiety and suffering.

Thought Regulator	
Mark Yes or No	
Can I control my thoughts?	
Can I change my thoughts?	
Can I think a problem through to the conclusion?	
Can I let something go, that I cannot control?	
Can I be quiet mentally?	
Can I sing and playfully enjoy my day?	

Lesson

Jesus is the Word. It is hard for Him to not have something to say. He is speaking to you and your ears will open to His voice as you learn to develop the Mind of Christ. *My sheep hear my voice, and I know them, and they follow me: and I give unto them eternal life; and they shall never perish, neither shall any man pluck them out of my hand. John 10:27-28KJV*

1) What kind of a mind does King David want his son, Solomon, to possess?

*And you, my son Solomon, acknowledge the God of your father, and serve him with wholehearted devotion and with a **willing mind**, for the LORD searches every heart and understands every motive behind the thoughts. 1 Chronicles 28:9*

2) What kind of a mind does a humble congregation possess?

*Also, in Judah the hand of God was on the people to give them **unity of mind** to carry out what the king and his officials had ordered, following the word of the Lord. 2 Chronicles 30:12*

3) What is David asking God to do for him?

*Test me, O LORD, and try me, **examine my heart and my mind**. Psalm 26:2*

4) Where do I need to focus my thoughts?

*You will keep in perfect peace, whose **mind is stayed on You (Lord)**: because he trusts in You. Isaiah 26:3KJV*

5) What does the Lord examine?

*I the LORD search the heart and **examine the mind**, to reward a man according to his conduct, according to what his deeds deserve. Jeremiah 17:10*

6) When we enter a covenant with the LORD, He places what in our minds?

*"I will put **my law in their minds** and **write it on their hearts**. I will be their God, and they will be my people." Jeremiah 31:33*

7) When Daniel followed the Lord with his whole heart, what kind of a mind did the Lord give him?

*This man Daniel, whom the king called Belteshazzar, was found to have a **keen mind** and knowledge and understanding and the ability to interpret dreams, explain riddles and solve difficult problems. Daniel 5:12*

8) What was Daniel's responsibility?

*"Do not be afraid, Daniel. Since the first day that you **set your mind to gain understanding** and to **humble yourself** before your God, your words were heard (prayed)..." Daniel 10:12*

9) What kind of a mind do you develop after an encounter with Jesus?

*When they came to Jesus, they saw the man who had been possessed by the legion of demons, sitting there, dressed and in his **right mind**, Mark 5:15*

10) When you walk with Jesus, what does He do for your mind?

*Then He **opened their minds** so they could understand the Scriptures. Luke 24:45*

11) When Paul testified about Jesus to those who did not believe what were the accusations towards him?

*At this point Festus interrupted Paul's defense. "**You are out of your mind**, Paul!" he shouted. "Your great learning is driving you **insane**." Acts 26:24*

12) How should we discipline our minds?
*I myself (Paul) in **my mind am a slave to God's law**...Romans 7:25*

13) How can we be transformed? *Do not conform any longer to the pattern of this world but be transformed by the **renewing of your mind**...Romans 12:2.*

14) In order to live in peace, we need to strive for what kind of mind?
*Be perfect (mature), be of good comfort, be of **one mind**, live in peace; and the God of love and peace shall be with you. 2 Corinthians 13:11KJV*

15) What are we commanded to do?
*You were taught with regard to your former life, to **put off your old self**, which is being corrupted by its deceitful desires; to **be made new in the attitudes of your minds**; and to **put on the new self**, created to be like God in true righteousness and holiness. Ephesians 4:22-24*

16)What is the helmet of salvation? *Take the helmet of salvation and the sword of the Spirit, which is the **Word of God**. Ephesians 6:17*

17) How can we make our joy complete? *...then make my joy complete by **being like-minded**, having the same love, being <u>one in spirit and purpose</u>. Philippians 2:2*

18) How do we keep from being consumed with earthly worries? ***Set your mind on things above***, *not on earthly things. Colossians 3:2*

19) When I mind my own business, what kind of a mind will I possess? *Make it your ambition to lead a **quiet** life, to mind your own business and to work with your hands... 1 Thessalonians 4:11*

20) What is our birthright as believers in Christ? *For God has not given us the spirit of fear; but of <u>power</u>, and of <u>love</u>, and of a **sound mind**. 2 Timothy 1:7*

21) What character traits do we need to develop to be like-minded? *Finally, all of you, live in harmony with one another; be **sympathetic**, <u>love as brothers</u>, be **compassionate and humble**. 1 Peter 3:8*

22) What kind of a mind is needed to defeat the devil and resist him and stand firm in the faith? *Be **sober, be vigilant**; because your adversary the devil, as a roaring lion, walks about, seeking whom he may devour; who resist steadfast in the faith...1 Peter 5:8-9KJV.*

Exercise

Discuss ways you could renew your mind.

Principle

A mature mind is quiet and peaceful.

Application

It takes maturity to develop right thinking skills. Right character needs to be developed alongside right thinking. The fruit of peace and quietness is a rich reward!

Mind of Christ

- Willingly serving God
- Unity with other believers
- Mind stayed on the Lord
- Examined for unbelief and sin
- Law of God on my mind
- Keen mind of understanding
- Set mind, humble mind
- Right mind
- Scriptures opened (illuminated) in your mind
- Disciplining self
- Renewing mind continually
- Protecting mind with the Word
- Setting our mind on things above
- Intentionally alert and sober

Character traits:

- Steadfast
- Loving
- Compassionate
- Sympathetic
- Humble

Fruit:

- Quiet
- Sound (self-disciplined) mind
- Peaceful
- Connected to other believers
- Able to resist evil
- Holy

Conclusion

Thoughts can be scattered, noisy and like unruly children. It is not until we take dominion of the ground between our ears that we can have peace. This is a battle! Disciplining our thinking and coaching ourselves into right thinking patterns is work. I must develop the mental strength to tell myself what I may and may not think. This is achievable. At first, it takes lots of effort, and then it will take a daily thought inventory and maintenance work. Maintaining healthy thinking is easier with practice. Now refuse stupid thoughts and choose what you will and will not think.

Set you mind on things above, not on earthly things.
Colossians 3:2

Lord, I grant you dominion over my thought life. Convict me over my entertaining negative thoughts and emotions of bitterness. Help me to intentionally put off the old and put on the new and to just let go of the past. Awaken my spirit that I may do these things. Amen.

LESSON 10

HEART OF CHRIST

I have hidden your word in my heart that I might not sin against you. Psalm 119:21

Introduction

A violin needs tuned before every performance. Our hearts need tuned every morning to the key of tenderness to receive love, joy, or peace. Otherwise, the dissonance of a stony heart will rule our lives with fearful anxiety, anger, or bitterness. In the parable of the seed and the sower, the stony heart develops no root. (Mark 4:16-18) Developing roots of courage, perseverance, diligence, strength, and steadfast stability require intentionality. Intentionally humbling ourselves before the Lord and allowing Him to give us a new heart. An old heart of stone is easily distracted, follows idols of the temporal, and cannot hold the glory of God.

Lesson

1) Here are the instructions: *Love the Lord your God with all your heart and with all your soul and with all your strength. Deuteronomy 6:5*

2) How do I love God like this? *These commandments that I give you today are to be upon your hearts. Deuteronomy 6:6*

3) How do I get the commandments on my heart? *...Talk about them when you lie down and when you get up. Tie them as symbols on your hands and bind them on your foreheads. Write them on the doorframes of your houses and on your gates. Deuteronomy 6:7-*

4) Why is this so important? *For as he thinks in his heart, so is he: Proverbs 23:7 (KJV)* Whatever we meditate or think on is what is coming out of our mouths.

5) How can I enjoy the blessings of a pure heart? *How can a young man keep his way pure? By living according to your word. I seek you with all my heart; do not let me stray from your commands. I have hidden your word in my heart that I might not sin against you. Psalm 119:9-11*

Exercise

Evaluate your heart.

HEART EVALUATION	
*Ezekiel 11:19-20; (19) I will give them **singleness of heart (undivided)** and put a **new spirit** within them; I will **take away** their <u>hearts of stone</u> and **give** them <u>tender hearts</u> instead, (20) so they will obey my laws and regulations. Then they will truly be my people, and I will be their God. (NLT)*	
TENDER HEART	**HEART OF STONE**
Upright/joyful heart Psalm 97:11	Hardened heart Exodus 4:21; 7:3, 13...
Heart free from sin Psalm 119:11	Stubborn/disloyal heart Psalm 78:8
Sound/blameless heart Psalm 119:80	Perverse heart Proverbs 12:8
Tried (tested) heart Jeremiah 17:10	Sorrowful heart Proverbs 15:13
Whole heart Jeremiah 24:7	Fretful/raging heart Proverbs 19:3
Single heart (undivided) Ezekiel 11:19	*Foolish heart Proverbs 22:15
Obedient heart Ezekiel 11:20	Wicked/evil heart Proverbs 26:23
*New heart Ezekiel 18:31	Fearful heart Isaiah 35:4
*New spirit/new heart Ezekiel 36:26	*Idolatrous heart Isaiah 44:15
*Spirit filled heart Ezekiel 36:27	Pagan heart Isaiah 44:16,17

Blessed heart Ezekiel 36:28	Blind/deluded heart Isaiah 44:18
Clean heart Ezekiel 36:29	Mindless heart Isaiah 44:19
Kept/guarded heart Proverbs 4:23	Deceived/deluded heart Isaiah 44:20
Honest/good heart Luke 8:15	Departing (Cursed) heart Jeremiah 17:5
Good heart=Fruitful life Luke 6:43	Desperately wicked heart Jeremiah 17:9
Wise heart Proverbs 10:8	Prideful heart Jeremiah 49:16
Believing heart Acts 8:37	Exiled heart Ezekiel 11:21
*Faithful heart Romans 10:6-9	*Unclean heart Matthew 15:18-19
Grateful heart (grace) Colossians 3:16	Simple easily deceived heart/mind Romans 16:18

Application

We must intentionally tune our ears to hear wisdom and apply our hearts to receive understanding. Proverbs says to call out for insight, cry aloud for understanding, look for wisdom as for silver and search for it as for hidden treasure, then we will understand the fear of the Lord and find the knowledge of God. (Proverbs 2:1-5) God's wisdom is not cheap or easy. It takes the pursuit of a diligent person to find it.

Principle

A happy heart is my responsibility to cultivate.

Conclusion

You cannot change your words, until you change your heart. *For out of the overflow of his heart his mouth speaks. Luke 6:45b*

Your heart is a mirror of what is going on inside of you. *As water reflects a face, so a man's heart reflects the man. Proverbs 27:19*

Your words reveal what is in your heart. *You brood of vipers, how can you who are evil say anything good? For out of the overflow of the heart the mouth speaks. Matthew 12:34*

The letters from Christ are written on our hearts. *You show that you are a letter from Christ, the result of our ministry, <u>written</u> not with ink but <u>with the Spirit of the living God</u>, not on tablets of stone but on tablets of human hearts. 2 Corinthians 3:3*

Christ is the light in our hearts to illuminate the way. *For God, who said, "Let light shine out of darkness," made his light shine in our hearts to give us the light of the knowledge of the glory of God in the face of Christ.* 2 Corinthians 4:6

Christ dwells in our hearts through faith. *So, Christ may dwell in your hearts through faith. Ephesians 3:17*

It is our duty to do the will of God from our hearts. *(Be like) slaves of Christ, doing the will of God from your heart. Ephesians 6:6*

The fruit of a tender heart is peace. *And the peace of God, which transcends all understanding, will guard your hearts and your minds in Christ Jesus. Philippians 4:7*

The Word of the Lord and other believers can encourage and comfort our hearts. *My purpose is that they may be encouraged in heart and united in love, so that they may have the full riches of complete understanding. Colossians 2:2*

After a time of testing, we will be strengthened, established, and settled in our hearts. *May he strengthen your hearts so that you will be blameless and holy in the presence of our God and Father when our Lord Jesus comes with all his holy ones.* 1 Thessalonians 3:13

Your instructions are to direct your heart into the love of God through perseverance and waiting upon Christ. *May the Lord direct your hearts into God's love and Christ's perseverance (patient waiting on Christ). 2 Thessalonians 3:5*

There are 884 verses In the Kings James Bible on the "heart". There is so much more for us to learn about our hearts. There are 30 verses on "heart" and the "wise".

| *A trained heart is a wise heart.*

For out of the overflow of the heart the mouth speaks.
Matthew 12:34

For this reason, I kneel before the Father, from whom his whole family in heaven and on earth derives its name. I pray that out of his glorious riches he may strengthen you with power through his Spirit in your inner being, so that Christ may dwell in your hearts through faith, and I pray that you, being rooted and established in love, may have power, together with all the saints, <u>to grasp how wide and long and high and deep is the love of Christ,</u> and to know this <u>love that surpasses knowledge</u>—that you may be filled to the measure of all the <u>fullness of God</u>. Now to him <u>who is able to do abundantly more</u> than all we ask or imagine, according to his power that is at work within us, to him be glory in the church and in Christ Jesus throughout all generations, for ever and ever! Amen Ephesians 3:14-20

LESSON 11

HIGHER AND LOWER LEVELS OF LOVE

Beloved means: one who is greatly loved.

Introduction

If there are no good examples of strong, healthy relationships in your past, be determined to break the cycle of unhealthy relationships now. Learn the higher levels of love and what love is and practice, practice, practice. Practice loving words, thoughts, and actions in everyday situations.

> *I can get my words and actions right, but the loving and kind thoughts have been the harder to master.*

Place the love is...love is never... list on the refrigerator and anyone who sounds demeaning, demanding, etc. Ask them: Is that love? We did this with our children and then sent them to the refrigerator to the list and let them take back their unloving words and exchange them for loving, kind speech. This made for a happy home and siblings that are still best friends. Foul speech can just be poor training and a bad habit.

> *Kindness training starts in the home.*

So, you say, is that being a hypocrite? No, it is not. It is the solid foundation of etiquette and good manners. It is designing a filter for my words and actions if I become emotionally unbalanced. If I do not feed the negativity, I can rebalance myself quicker with less of a mess to clean up.

> Emotional imbalances cause deep wounds if I indulge the accompanying noxious negative thinking.

Developmental Stages of Love

Lower levels of love

1. **Self-love** – empty, lonely, using others. Characterized by a life of confusion.

   People will be lovers of themselves, lovers of money, boastful, proud, abusive, disobedient to their parents, ungrateful, unholy, without love, unforgiving, slanderous, without self-control, brutal, not lovers of the good, treacherous, rash, conceited, lovers of pleasures rather than lovers of God – having a form of godliness but denying its power. Have nothing to do with them. 2 Timothy 3:2-5

2. **False Love** – kind speech in mouth, but not in heart. This type of love is very irritating.

   If I speak in the tongues of men and of angels, but have not love, I am only a resounding gong or a clanging cymbal. 1 Corinthians 13:1

3. **Enabling Love** – This person understands consequences and tries to remove the mountains in other people's lives. Most usually these mountains are particularly important so that the person can grow and mature and become strong. This person has faith, but their faith is usually in themselves or in their money.

   If I have a gift of prophecy and can fathom all mysteries and all knowledge, and If I have a faith that can move mountains, but have not love, I am nothing. 1 Corinthians 13:2

4. **Best Effort Love** – This person does a lot of charity work and gives of themselves. They do this to look good or to make up for other things in their lives that are not right. This type of love can be motivated by guilt or a need for approval and acceptance.

If I give all I possess to the poor and surrender my body to the flames, but have not love, I gain nothing. 1 Corinthians 13:3

Higher levels of love: Understanding my purpose in life!

5. **True Love** – Patient and Kind. This person wrestles their own stubborn self-will and pins it to the ground and pursues being a person that loves this way. **This person repents often.**

    Love is patient, love is kind. It does not envy, it does not boast, it is not proud. It is not rude, it is not self-seeking, it is not easily angered, it keeps no record of wrongs. Love does not delight in evil but rejoices with the truth. It always protects, always trusts, always hopes, always perseveres.

    Love never fails. 1 Corinthians 13:4-8a

6. **Tough love** – This love is strong enough to allow others to have their own free will and make their own choices and suffer their own consequences. This person trust that others can find their own path.

    I urge you, brothers, to watch out for those who cause divisions and put obstacles in your way that are contrary to the teaching you have learned. Keep away from them. Romans 16:17-19

7. **Perfect Love** – Characterized by having no fear. Speaks truth to himself frequently and wrestles fears and pins them to the ground.

    There is no fear in love. But perfect love drives out fear because fear has to do with punishment (torment). 1 John 4:18

8. **Love your Higher Power and your neighbor as yourself.** This love is pure and seeks opportunity to help those in genuine need.

    Jesus replied: "Love the Lord your God with all your heart and with all your soul and with all your mind. This is the first and greatest commandment. And the second is like it: Love your neighbor as yourself. All the Law and the Prophets hang on these two commandments." Matthew 22:37-40

9. **Love with great peace** – This person will never take an offense. But he will instead, bear the burden of others. This person visits the sick and makes meals for those with cancer or a new baby. This person keeps their schedule loose enough to plan for the little interruptions in life.

    Great peace have they who love your law, and nothing can make them stumble (offended). Psalm 119:165; Carry each other's burdens, and in this way, you will fulfill the law of Christ. Galatians 6:2

10. **Everlasting love** – This love transcends time, space and all eternity and will love forever. This is a love that is more powerful than life. This is a place of safety and honor. When there is a higher level of faithful, devoted, selfless reciprocal love and devotion, you can be greatly loved and find someone you can greatly love and be someone's beloved.

...I have loved you with an everlasting love; I have drawn you with loving-kindness. Jeremiah 31:3

Finding mature love means letting go of the lower levels of love. This will allow you to give and receive higher levels of love.

Exercise

What would your life look like if you operated in the higher levels of love?

Application

Think Effective Boundaries – At times, you may need to draw near your loved ones. At other times, you may need to move back from them to allow them space to work through the developmental stages of love. We can love the person and hate their behavior. *Be merciful to those who doubt; snatch others from the fire and save them; to others show mercy, mixed with fear—hating even the clothing stained by corrupted flesh. Jude 22-23*

If you expect mature devoted love, you must be a whole enough person to receive it.

Principle

There is a time to love, and a time to hate. Ecclesiastes 3:1

Conclusion

When working with immature people with lower levels of love, use boundaries to choose loving responses. Do not mirror poor behaviors, instead use cognitive reasoning to resolve to love others by allowing them to experience the consequences of their own poor choices.

Lower levels of love cause suffering. Suffering, if we accept it, can work us into the higher levels of love at a faster pace. There is an open mature heart that recognizes what "love is..." and embraces it and refuses what "love is never..." and rejects it. *We have spoken freely to you, Corinthians, and opened wide our hearts to you. 2 Corinthians 6:11*

We have spoken freely to you, Corinthians, and opened wide our hearts to you. 2 Corinthians 6:11

Love is...Love is Never!

Love is....	Love is never....
Peaceful	Demeaning
Gentle	Demanding
Kind	Abusive
Rewarding	Neglectful
Caring	Manipulative
Sharing	Hateful/Selfish
Patient	Argumentative
Forgiving	Vengeful
Always wanting best for others	Controlling; demanding own way
Working it out together	Fearful
Talking it out together	Full of should & should ...not
Respectful	Resentful/Bitter
Trusting	Accusatory
Forgetting the past	Never forgetting the ...past/shaming
Giving and Helping	Selfish/self-centered
Always thinking of how to encourage others	Discouraging
Always uplifts another	Tearing down the esteem ...of another
Allows freedom to choose	Yelling and angry

Allows person to receive consequences for poor choices.	Manipulates other people ...emotionally and bullies ...to get them to do what ...they want
Hopes for the best	Denies there is a problem
Refuses emotional manipulation	Accepts consequences or ...interrupts the (enabler)
Gets wise counsel, ponders each word spoken and each deed done.	Decisions based on ...emotions
Seeks help for self when ...stuck emotionally	Throws money at a ...problem to "fix it"
Sets standard and a plan	Makes excuses for ...themselves and others
Sticks to the plan ...Accountable	Smooths things over
...Willing to suffer for right ...decisions	Hides things
Willing to avoid rebellious ...people if needed	Everyone must get along ...at all costs
Always kind, but firm	Easily manipulated
Backs up words with actions	Angry
Always does the next right ...thing	Anxious
Is not manipulative and ...does not manipulate	Confused
Holds others accountable	Poor boundaries
Committed to doing what is ...right	Chaos
Respects individuality	Dominate and controlling
Harmonious	Passive and Double- ...minded
Teachable	Not interested in learning
Gentle	Prideful

Lord grant me freedom from lower levels of love. Let me not practice them on others. Let me not accept lower levels of love from others Let me practice what love is... every day. Let me repent quickly when I use unloving words or behaviors. Especially if I am excusing them and calling them love. This I pray in your name. Amen.

LESSON 12

JOYFULNESS

...In your presence is fullness of joy, and at your right hand there are pleasures for evermore. Psalm 16:11

Introduction

Joyfulness is a happy countenance which comes from being in the presence of the Lord. We can be joyful and sorrowful at the same time. Joy is a condition of the Spirit and sorrow is a condition of the soul. *...sorrowful, yet always rejoicing; poor, yet making many rich; having nothing, and yet possessing everything. 2 Corinthians 6:10*

Lesson

Things that Increase Joy
1) **Clear Conscience** For our ***rejoicing***_is this, the testimony of our (clear)\conscience, that in simplicity and godly sincerity, not with fleshly wisdom, but by the grace of God... 2 Corinthians 1:12
2) **Precepts/Statutes** The precepts of the LORD are right, giving ***joy*** to the heart. Psalms 19:8
3) **Obey commands** (10) If you obey my commands, you will remain in my love... (11) I have told you this so that my ***joy*** may be in you and that your joy may be complete. (12) My command is this: Love each other as I have loved you. John 15:10-12

4) Abide in His Words *If you remain in me and my words remain in you, ask whatever you wish, and it will be given you. I have told you this so that my joy may be in you and that your **joy** may be complete. John 15:7,11*

5) Finding God's Words *When your words came, I ate them, they were my joy and my heart's delight. Jeremiah 15:16*

6) Right Words *A man finds **joy** in giving an apt reply—and how good is a timely word! Proverbs 15:23*

Things that Diminish our Joy

1) Broken Heart *Restore to me the **joy** of your salvation and grant me a willing spirit, to sustain me. Psalm 51:12*

2) Walking in Darkness *We write this to make your **joy** complete... God is light and in Him is no darkness at all. 1 John 1:4-5*

3) Iniquity in my heart blocks fellowship with the Lord *If I had cherished sin (darkness, cursing, death) in my heart, the Lord would not have listened. Psalm 66:18*

4) Un-forgiveness *But if you do not forgive men their sin, your Father will not forgive your sins. Matthew 6:14*

Tests to Produce Joy

Insults, persecutions, false accusations, all kinds of evil things *(11) Blessed are you when people insult you, persecute you and falsely say all kinds of evil against you because of me. (12) **Rejoice** and be glad, because great is your reward in heaven, for in the same way they persecuted the prophets who were before you. Matthew 5:11-12*

Why would our faith be tested?

Perseverance *(2) Consider it pure joy, my friends, whenever you face trials of many kinds, (3) because you know that the testing of your faith develops perseverance. (4) Perseverance must finish its work so that you may be **mature and complete**, not lacking anything. James 1:2-4*

Reasons to Rejoice

Name written in Heaven *However, do not rejoice that the spirits submit to you, but **rejoice** that your names are written in heaven. Luke 10:20*

It is the POWER of the Holy Spirit *(22) But the fruit of the Spirit is love, **joy**, peace, patience, kindness, goodness, faithfulness, (23) gentleness and self-control. Against such things there is no law. Galatians 5:22*

What are the Steps to Rejoicing

- Outline Psalm 105:1-5
- **Give** thanks
- **Call** upon His name
- **Make known** His deeds
- **Sing** praise to Him
- **Glory** in His name
- Let your heart **rejoice**
- **Seek** the Lord and His strength.
- **Remember** His marvelous works

Mature Thinking Skills

Our response is to **give thanks**, because giving thanks is an act of obedience. It is not an emotion. *Give thanks in all circumstances, for this is God's will for you in Christ Jesus. 1 Thessalonians 5:18*

- **All things Come from God.** *"Naked I came from my mother's womb, and naked I will depart. The Lord gave and the Lord has taken away; may the name of the Lord be praised." Job 1:21; Are not two sparrows sold for a penny? Yet not one of them will fall to the ground apart from the will of your Father. Matthew 10:29*

- **All things work together for good.** *And we know that in all things God works for the good of those who love him, who have been called according to his purpose. Romans 8:28*

- **Every circumstance can build character.** *For those God foreknew he also predestined to be conformed to the likeness of his Son, that he might be the firstborn among many brothers. Romans 8:29*

- **Difficulties and afflictions can teach us God's ways.** *It was good for me to be afflicted so that I might learn your decrees. Psalm 119:71*

What to do in times of trouble?

Crying Out *Call to me and I will answer you and tell you great and unsearchable things you do not know. Jeremiah 33:3*

Spirit-Filled

1) **Singing** *Speak to one another with psalms, hymns, and spiritual songs. Sing and make music in your heart to the Lord. Ephesians 5:19*

> 2) **Fullness of His Presence** *You have made known to me the path of life; you will fill me with joy in your presence, with eternal pleasures at your right hand. Psalm 16:11*

Rejoice Response to Suffering

> But ***rejoice*** *that you are insulted because of the name of Christ, you are blessed, for the Spirit of glory and of God rests on you. 1 Peter 4:13*

Greatest Joy

> **Hear Children** *I have no greater **joy** than to hear my children are walking in the truth. 3 John 4*

> **Well done** *His Lord said unto him, well done, good and faithful servant: you have been faithful over a few things, I will make you ruler over many things: enter into the joy of the Lord. Matthew 25:21*

Exercise

What part of this lesson spoke to you the most?

Application

Joy gives us strength. *Do not grieve, for the joy of the LORD is your strength. Nehemiah 8:10*

Joy is our health. *A cheerful heart is good medicine, but a crushed spirit dries up the bones. Proverbs 17:22*

Joy brings happiness. *A happy heart makes the face cheerful, but heartache crushes the spirit. Proverbs 15:13*

Principle

Joy gives strength, health, and happiness.

Conclusion

Joy is allusive. It will hide behind problems.

The ability to express and feel joy is connected to the ability
to feel painful emotions and release them quickly.

Joy must be an intentional pursuit. Anxiety, fear, and stress is in the soul or that earthly, fleshly part of ourselves. Anxiety is always a thief coming to kill, steal and destroy (John 10:10) We must pursue higher ground by intentionally walking in the fruit of the Spirit of Joy.

At his tabernacle will I sacrifice with shouts of joy, I will
sing and make music to the Lord. Psalm 27:6b

Lord when my joy is allusive remind me to go and search for her. Let me hold onto this precious gift of joy. May You always give me the oil of gladness instead of mourning, and a garment of praise instead of a spirit of despair. Would You make me an oak of righteousness? That I may display the splendor of the Lord. (Isaiah 61:3)

LESSON 13

PEACE

*Love the Lord your God with all your heart and with all your
soul and with all your strength and with all your mind and love
your neighbour as yourself. Luke 10:27*

Introduction

The problem with maintaining peace is that we shift our focus onto people, possessions, or positions to do for us what only God can do. If we expect someone or something else to meet our inner needs this is idolatry.

Idolatry always leaves us empty and anxious.

Soon, we are full of exaggerated emotions. For example, if I expect my spouse to meet all my needs and he, of course, is not able to do this, I am likely to throw him off the throne of my heart and step on and crush him. He was never meant to be on the throne that is a place reserved for God. There is no spouse, mate, children, church, job, career, education, house, ministry, etc. that can ever rule my heart with peace, only God can do that. First, let us look at unity that can result in peace, next some obstacles to peace and finally how to respond to attacks and finding lasting peace through the Holy Spirit.

Lasting peace only comes from fellowship with the God.

Lesson

Unity that results in peace

1) **The Lord Jesus prays for us to be in one-accord with Him and the Father and each other.** *...I pray...that all of them may be one, Father just as you are in me and I am in you. May they also be in us so that the world may believe that you sent me. I have given them the glory that you gave me, that they may be one as we are one. John 17:20-22*

2) **Pray to have like-minded friends.** *...then make my joy complete by being like-minded, having the same love, being in one spirit and purpose. Philippians 2:2* Intentionally look around and find the people who are seeking the Lord and need support and encouragement.

3) **Walk with those in the light and not in darkness.** *But if we walk in the light, we have fellowship with one another, and the blood of Jesus, his Son, purifies us from all sin. 1 John 1:7*

4) **Unity among family, friends, churches, and co-workers is pleasant**. *How good and pleasant it is when brothers dwell in unity. Psalm 133:1*

5) **Learn to be spiritually minded.** *The mind of a sinful man is death, but the mind controlled by the Spirit is life and peace. Romans 8:6*

6) **We are justified through faith and have peace with God by grace.** *Therefore, since we have been justified through faith, we have peace with God through our Lord Jesus Christ, through whom we have gained access by faith into this grace in which we now stand. Romans 5:1-2*

Obstacles to lasting peace.

1) **Does not matter how many people agree with you, if you are wrong, you are wrong.** *Though hand join in hand, the wicked shall not be unpunished. Proverbs 11:21KJV*

2) **Seek out advice. Look for your pride if you are quarreling or contentious.** *Pride only breeds quarrels, but wisdom is found in those who take advice. Proverbs 13:10*

3) **The Lord does not bless self-promotion.** *...let us build us a city and a tower... let us make a name for ourselves...so the Lord scattered them...Genesis 11:4,8 KJV*

4) **A talebearer or gossip will not have peace.** *A gossip betrays a confidence, but a trustworthy man keeps a secret. Proverbs 11:13. ...without a gossip a quarrel dies down. Proverbs 26:20 The words of a talebearer are as wounds, and they go down into the innermost parts of the belly. Proverbs 26:22KJV* Instructions *...Avoid a man that talks too much. Proverbs 20:19*

5) **Do not be a meddler/busybody**. If you suffer, it should not be as a murderer or thief or any other kind of criminal, or even as a meddler (busybody). 1 Peter 4:15

6) Do not be conceited and think you are better than others. *Live in harmony with one another. Do not be proud but be willing to associate with people of low position. Do not be conceited. Romans 12:16*

Response to False Accusers

1) How did Stephen respond to a gang attacking him in one-accord? *Then they cried out with a loud voice, and stopped their ears, and ran upon him with one accord. Acts 7:57 While they were stoning him, Stephen prayed, "Lord, Jesus, receive my spirit." Then he fell on his knees and cried out, "Lord, do not hold this sin against them." ... Acts 7:59-60.*

2) How did Jesus respond at his crucifixion? *When they came to the place called the Skull, there they crucified him, along with the criminals... Jesus said, "Father, forgive them, for they do not know what they are doing." And then they divided up his clothes by casting lots. Luke 23:33-34*

Exercise

What wound/offense is robbing your peace?

Application

Sometimes, there is nothing to do with evil than to forgive it. Jesus made the first move to show us spiritual maturity through righteousness and peace. *But God demonstrates his own love for us in this: While we were still sinners, Christ died for us. Romans 5:8*

Understand that Jesus is peace, and he gives peace to believers, *Peace I leave with you; my peace I give you. I do not give to you as the world gives. Do not let your hearts be troubled and do not be afraid. John 14:27* But he did not come to bring peace between unrighteousness and righteousness. *Do not suppose that I have come to bring peace to the earth. I did not come to bring peace, but a sword. For I have come to turn a man against his father, a daughter against her mother, a daughter-in-law against her mother-in-law—a man's enemies will be the members of his own household. Matthew 10:34-36*

Principle

Walking in peace is my responsibility.

Conclusion

Believers have an opportunity to live supernaturally in the power of the Holy Spirit to be overcomers. *For the kingdom of God... is righteousness, peace, and joy in the Holy Spirit. Romans 14:17* Here are the comforting words of Jesus: *I have told you these things, so that in me you may have peace. In this world you will have trouble. But take heart! I have overcome the world.* Do what is right. Walk in peace and hold onto your joy!

Blessing: May the God of hope fill you with all joy and peace as you trust in him, so that you may overflow with hope by the power of the Holy Spirit. Romans 15:13

Lord teach me to bless others and not to curse. Teach me to walk in the shoes of peace and to guard peace like the blessed treasure that it is. Bless me, O Lord, bless me with everlasting peace. Amen

LESSON 14

PATIENCE

You too, be patient and stand firm, because the Lord's
coming is near. James 5:8

Introduction

Patience is bearing pain or trials calmly and without complaint; manifesting forbearance under provocation or strain; not hasty or impetuous; steadfast despite opposition, difficulty, or adversity. A patient person is slow to anger, longsuffering, persevering, waiting, cheerful and hopeful. Patience does not develop on its own; it is an intentional practice. We must intentionally put on patience and take off impatience.

Lesson

1. **The opposite of a patient attitude is a prideful attitude. Impatience is displayed in anger. Anger is equated to foolishness.** *...the patient in spirit is better than the proud in spirit. 9 Be not hasty in your spirit to be angry: for anger rests in the bosom of fools. Ecclesiastes 7:8*

2. **Contentious and self-seeking is the opposite of patience. If we are contentious, we will receive indignation, wrath, tribulation, anguish, and evil works. This is not because God is unloving, but because He renders to every man according to his deeds. A patient person is promised glory, honor, immortality, and eternal life.** <u>Penitent </u>– repentant; impenitent mean unrepentant.

Romans 2:5-8 But after thy hardness and impenitent heart treasure up unto thyself wrath against the day of wrath and revelation of the righteous judgment of God; 6 who will render to every man according to his deeds: 7 to them who by patient continuance in well doing seek for glory and honor , immortality, eternal life; 8 but unto them that are contentious and do not obey the truth, but obey unrighteousness, indignation and wrath, 9 tribulation and anguish upon every soul of man that doeth evil, of the Jew first, and also of the Gentile; 10 but glory, honor, and peace, to every man that works good....

3. *Romans 12:9 Let love be without dissimulation. Abhor that which is evil; cleave to that which is good. 10 Be kindly affectioned one to another with brotherly love; in honor preferring one another; 11 not slothful in business; fervent in spirit; serving the Lord; 12 rejoicing in hope; patient in tribulation; continuing instant in prayer...*

Dissimulation *- to hide under false appearance (hypocrisy).*

What does it look like to serve the Lord?

Christian Service to the Lord
A. Love without hypocrisy
B. Hate evil
C. Cleave to the good
D. Kind to one another
E. Thinking of others before yourself
F. Not Lazy
G. Fervent- sincere deep emotion
H. Rejoicing in hope
I. Patient in our troubles
J. Always prayerful

4. *Romans 12: 13 distributing to the necessity of saints; given to hospitality, 14 Bless them which persecute you; bless, and curse not. 15 Rejoice with them that do rejoice, and weep with them that weep. 16 Be of the same mind one towards another. Mind not high things but condescend to men of low estate. Be not wise in your own conceits. 17 Recompense to no man evil for evil. Provide things honest in the sight of all men. 18 if it be possible, as much as lies in you, live peaceably with all men. 19 Dearly beloved, avenge not yourselves, but rather give place unto wrath: for it is written, Vengeance is mine; I will repay, says the Lord. 20 Therefore if your enemy hunger, feed him; if he thirsts, give him drink; for in so doing, you shall heap coals of fire on his head. 21 Be not overcome of evil but overcome evil with good.*

What would a mature Christian look like who cannot be overpowered by evil?

Instructions for Mature Christianity
A. Giving to others
B. Hospitable
C. Learning to bless those who persecute you.
D. Compassionate to others
E. One accord (unity) with other believers
F. Living in peace with others (as much as possible)
G. No respects of persons
H. Not conceited—not having an excessively high opinion of yourself.
I. Not vengeful—punish or inflict
J. Trusting God to avenge you, if necessary
K. Being extra kind to your enemy
L. Overcoming evil with good
M. Feed your enemy and give him something to drink

5. *I Thessalonians 5: 12 And we beseech you, brethren, to know them which labor among you, and are over you in the Lord, and admonish you: 13 and to esteem them very highly in love for their work's sake and be at peace among yourselves. 14 now we exhort you, brethren, warn them that are unruly, comfort the feebleminded, support the weak, be patient toward all men. 15 See that none render evil for evil unto any man; but ever follow that which is good, both among yourselves, and to all men. 16 Rejoice evermore, 17 Pray without ceasing. 18 in everything give thanks: for this is the will of God in Christ Jesus concerning you. 19 Quench not the Spirit. 20 Despise not prophesyings. 21 Prove all things; hold fast that which is good. 22 Abstain from all appearance of evil. **Prayer:** 23 And the very God of peace sanctify you wholly; and I pray God your whole spirit and soul and body be preserved blameless unto the coming of our Lord Jesus Christ. **Promise** 24 Faithful is he that calleth you, who also will do it.*

What are the instructions?
A. Know and highly respect those who instruct us
B. Be at peace among yourself as much as possible
C. Exhort (encourage) each other
D. Warn the unruly
E. Support the faint hearted–those lacking in courage or resolution, timid
F. Support the weak
G. Be patient toward all men

H. Do not render evil for evil unto any man
I. Follow that which is good
J. Rejoice
K. Pray without ceasing
L. Give thanks in everything (This is the will of God.)
M. Quench not the Spirit (extinguish, put out, smother, choke, rub out)
N. Despise not preaching (prophesying)
O. Test all things. Choose the good.
P. Abstain from evil.

6. *2 Thessalonians 3:3 But the Lord is faithful, who shall establish you, and keep you from evil. 4 And we have confidence in the Lord touching you, that you both do and will do the things which we command you. 5 And the Lord direct your hearts into the love of God and into the patient waiting for Christ.*

Established in Christ	
1. What is God's character like?	Faithful
2. What will God do for us?	Establish us and keep us from evil
3. What kind of attitude should we possess?	Confident
4. Who directs our hearts if we are obedient?	God
5. Where will God direct our hearts?	Into the "love of God"
6. How should we respond?	With patient waiting for Christ

7. *I Timothy 3:1 This is a true saying, if a man desires the office of a bishop, he desires a good work. 2 A bishop then must be blameless, the husband of one wife, vigilant, sober, of good behavior, given to hospitality, apt to teach; 3 not given to wine, no striker, not greedy of filthy lucre; but patient, not a brawler, not covetous, 4 one that rules well his own house, having his children in subjection with all gravity... 6 Not a novice, lest being lifted up with <u>pride</u> he falls into condemnation of the devil. 7 Moreover he must have a good report of them which are without; lest he fall into reproach and the snare of the devil.*

What are the qualifications of a godly leader?
• Desires good work
• Blameless
• Husband/wife of one mate
• Vigilant–alertly watchful to avoid danger
• Sober marked by an earnest thoughtful character; unhurried, calm with self-control
• Good behavior
• Hospitable given to generous and cordial reception of guest
• Apt to teach
• Not one who uses strong drink
• Not a striker–to aim and deliver a blow or thrust with a weapon, hand or tool
• Not greedy
• **PATIENT**
• Not a brawler–to quarrel or fight noisily
• Not covetous (marked by an inordinate desire for wealth or possessions or for another's possessions).
• Rules his own house well
1. What is the sin nature a novice must conquer? Pride
2. Where will pride lead us? Pride leads to condemnation as the devil.
3. If we have not protected our reputation and we fall into reproach what happens? We are in the snare of the devil.

8. *2 Timothy 2:24-26 And the servant of the Lord must not strive; but be gentle unto all men, apt to teach, patient, 25 In meekness instructing those that oppose themselves; if God peradventure will give them repentance to the acknowledging of the truth; 26 And that they may recover themselves out of the snare of the devil, who are taken captive by him at his will.*

How to Recover from the Snare of the Devil	
A. Who are we?	Servants of the Lord
B. What are we not to do?	Strive with others
C. What is the opposite of striving?	Gentle, apt to teach, **patient**
D. How are we to teach and instruct others?	In meekness (humility)
E. Why?	Because perhaps God will lead them to the truth and

	repentance
F. What do we need to recover from?	The snare of the devil.
G. When we do not know or follow truth, who can take us captive?	The devil
H. What is it like when the devil takes us captive?	It is like being in a trap.

9. *James 5:7 Be patient therefore, brethren, unto the coming of the Lord. Behold, the farmer waits for the precious fruit of the earth, and hath long patience for it, until he receives the early and the latter rain. 8 Be ye also patient; establish your hearts: for the coming of the Lord draws nigh. 9 Grudge (grumble) not one against another, brethren, lest you be condemned: behold, the judge stands before the door. 10 Take, my brethren, the prophets, who have spoken in the name of the Lord, for an example of suffering affliction, and of patience. 11 Behold, we count them happy (blessed) which endure. Ye have heard of the patience of Job and have seen the end of the Lord; that the Lord is very pitiful, and of tender mercy.*

Instructions from James	
A. Patient for what?	The coming of the Lord
B. Like who?	The farmer
C. What are we waiting for?	Precious fruit
D. What kind of patience do we need?	Long
E. While we are waiting what will be our temptation?	Grumbling
F. What does God say will happen if we grumble?	We will be condemned.
G. Who was our examples?	Prophets were patient in suffering and affliction.
H. Who is happy?	Those who endure like Job.
I. How will God respond to us if we are **patient**?	Very pitiful and of tender mercy.

10. *I Peter 18 Servants, be subject to your masters with all fear (reverence); not only to the good and gentle, but also to the forward. 19 For this is thankworthy (commendable), if a man for conscience toward God endure grief, suffering wrongfully. 20 For what glory is it, if when you be buffeted (beaten) for your faults, you shall take it patiently? But if, when you do well, and suffer for it, you take it patiently, this is acceptable with God. 21 For even hereunto*

were you called: because Christ also suffered for us, leaving us an example, that you should follow his steps: 22 Who did no sin, neither was guile (deceit) found in his mouth: 23 Who when he was reviled, reviled not again; when he suffered, he threatened not; but committed himself to him that judges righteously; 24 Who his own self bare our sins in his own body on the tree, that we, being dead to sins, should live unto righteousness: By whose stripes you were healed. 25 For you were sheep going astray; but are now returned unto the Shepherd and Bishop (overseer) of our souls.

Instructions from Peter	
A. Who are we to be subject to?	Masters (authorities; parents, teachers, government leaders, police, employers)
B. What is our attitude to be like towards our masters?	Fear (reverence)
C. What is commendable before God?	Enduring grief while suffering wrongfully.
D. Should we suffer patiently when corrected for our own wrongdoing?	Yes
E. Is there any glory when we suffer for our own wrongdoing?	No
F. Where is the glory?	When we suffer for well doing.
G. Who else suffered patiently when he was wronged?	Christ
H. How should we respond when we suffer wrongfully?	Like Christ; patiently, with no mouth of deceit or guile, not reviling, not threatening, but committing ourselves to God.
I. Why would Christ suffer patiently?	To take away our sins.
J. What are we dead to?	Sin
K. How are we to live?	In Righteousness
L. Why?	Because we are healed (Healed from impatience and pride?)
M. When we are patient with afflictions who will keep us from going astray and be our Shepherd?	Christ
N. Shepherd of what?	Our souls

Exercise

Where do you need more patience?

Application

When our spirit comes alive to Christ our soul can be healed from all past traumas. Our emotions will stop controlling us; and our minds will be at peace knowing we are in the will of God and our "self-will" will be purposed to be dead to sin... living in righteousness. Learn the habit of being patient. Humble yourself and go back and repent when you are impatient. Love is patient.

Principle

Patience makes others feel loved.

Conclusion

There are eternal rewards for patience and heartache with impatience. We are to be always patient with everyone. Patience exhibits maturity.

| *Patient is opposite of pride and anger.*

Without patience towards others, they may not recover themselves from the devil's snares. Impatience could set our own selves up for the devil's trap. We are to patiently wait on the Lord. Patience is a character trait and example from Job, the prophets, and Christ for us to follow. Patience is a fruit of the Spirit and the first example of love.

Love is patient, love is kind. 1 Corinthians 13:4

Lord, let patience be my expression of love. Teach me to love others with great patience. Let all frustration, irritation and impatience be put away from me. Especially when I am with children. Amen

LESSON 15

GENTLENESS/GOODNESS/ KINDNESS

...follow after righteousness, godliness, faith, love, endurance, and gentleness. Fight the good fight of the faith. Take hold of the eternal life which you were called... 1 Timothy 6:11-12

Introduction

Gentleness is the good fight of the faith for spiritual maturity. *Gentleness, goodness and kindness are the opposite of harshness, bullying and abusive. Unless we nurture ourselves and those around us, we will not be able to reach our full potential.*

| *Godly character keeps us from being ineffective and unproductive.*

(7) For this very reason, make every effort to add to your faith goodness; and to goodness, knowledge; and to knowledge, self-control; and to self-control, perseverance; and to perseverance, godliness; and to godliness, brotherly kindness; and to brotherly kindness, love. (8) For if you possess these qualities in increasing measure, they will <u>keep you from being ineffective and unproductive</u> in your knowledge of our Lord Jesus Christ. (9) But if anyone does not have them, he is <u>nearsighted and blind</u> and has <u>forgotten</u> that he has been <u>cleansed from his past sins</u>. 2 Peter 1:7-9

Lesson

Gentleness

1) **A gentle person is easy to approach, available and teachable.** ... _wisdom_ that comes from heaven is first of all pure; then peace-loving, considerate, submissive, full of mercy and good fruit, impartial and sincere. James 3:16

2) **Gentle words promote peace.** A gentle answer turns away wrath, but a harsh word stirs up anger. Proverbs 15:1 Actions always speak louder than words. Not only do my actions need to match my words, but if my tone and attitude is not right, I will be rejected.

3) **The Lord is a gentle shepherd.** The Lord is my shepherd, I shall not be in want. Psalm 23:1 He tends his flock like a shepherd: He gathers the lambs in his arms and carries them close to his heart; he gently leads those that have young. Isaiah 40:11 **You cannot harshly drive sheep or children.** ... "My lord knows that the children are tender and that I must care for the ewes and cows that are nursing their young. If they are driven hard just one day, all the animals will die." Genesis 33:13

4) **Gentle care is like a mother with little children.** ...but we were gentle among you, like a mother caring for her little children. We loved you so much that we were delighted to share with you not only the gospel of God but our lives as well, because you had become so dear to us. 1 Thessalonians 2:7-8

5) **Gentleness makes us great!** David speaks of the Lord's gentleness with him. ... And thy gentleness has made me great. Psalm 18:35KJV

Goodness

6) **Speak evil of no one.** ... do whatever is good, slander no one, be peaceable and considerate, and show true humility to all men. Titus 3:2

7) **Overcome evil with good.** Do not be overcome by evil but overcome evil with good. Romans 12:21

8) **Taste the goodness of the Lord.** Taste and see that the LORD is good; blessed is the man who takes refuge in him. Psalm 34:8

9) **Trust and do good.** Trust in the Lord and do good; dwell in the land and enjoy safe pasture. Psalm 37:3

11) **A good man's steps are ordered.** *The steps of a good man are ordered by the LORD: And he delights in his way. Psalm 37:23KJV*

Kindness

12) **The law is kindness.** *She opens her mouth with wisdom; and in her tongue is the law of kindness. Proverbs 31:26*

13) **God is kind.** *But you are a forgiving God, gracious and compassionate, slow to anger and abounding in love (great kindness). Nehemiah 9:17*

14) **Kindness and Compassion are best friends.** *Be kind and compassionate to one another, forgiving each other, just as in Christ God forgave you. Ephesians 4:32*

Exercise

Choose the most chaotic hour of your day and practice gentleness, goodness, and kindness.

Application

This is the steps to walking out gentleness, goodness, and kindness with love.

Instructions for Sincere Love and Kindness
• Love must be sincere.
• Hate what is evil.
• Cling to what is good.
• Be devoted to each other in brotherly love.
• Honor one another above yourselves.
• Keep spiritual fervor, serving the Lord.
• Be joyful in hope.
• Be patient in affliction.
• Be faithful in prayer.
• Share with those in need.
• Practice hospitality.
• Bless those who persecute you.
• Rejoice with those who rejoice.
• Mourn with those who mourn.
• Live in harmony with one another.

• Associate with people of low position.
• Be careful to do what is right.
• Live at peace with everyone, as much as possible.
• If your enemy is hungry, feed him.
• If your enemy is thirsty, give him something to drink.
• Overcome evil with good.

Do Not's
• Do not lack zeal.
• Do not curse others.
• Do not be proud.
• Do not be conceited.
• Do not repay evil for evil.
• Do not take revenge.
• Be not overcome by evil.

Romans 12:9-21 (9) Love must be sincere. Hate what is evil; cling to what is good. (10) Be devoted to one another in brotherly love, Honor one another above yourselves. (11) Never be lacking in zeal, but keep your spiritual fervor, serving the Lord. (12) Be joyful in hope, patient in affliction, faithful in prayer. (13) Share with God's people who are in need. Practice hospitality. (14) Bless those who persecute you; bless and do not curse. (15) Rejoice with those who rejoice; mourn with those who mourn. (16) Live in harmony with one another. Do not be proud but be willing to associate with people of low position. Do not be conceited. (17) Do not repay anyone evil for evil. Be careful to do what is right in the eyes of everybody. (18) If it is possible, as far as it depends on you, live at peace with everyone. (19) Do not take revenge, my friends, but leave room for God's wrath, for it is written: "It is mine to avenge; I will repay." Says the Lord, (20) On the contrary: "If your enemy is hungry, feed him; if he is thirsty, give him something to drink. In doing this, you will heap burning coals on his head." (21) Do not be overcome by evil but overcome evil with good.

Principle

Gentleness, goodness, and kindness is part of the heavenly wisdom.

Conclusion

The Lord is gentle, good, and kind. *Your gentleness makes us great. Psalm 18:35; O give thanks to the Lord; for he is good... 1 Chronicles 16:34; ... but with everlasting kindness I will have mercy on you... Isaiah 54:10.* As we walk with the Lord, we will become like him. Gentleness, goodness, and kindness comes naturally to no one. These are character traits that must be intentionally cultivated. Trauma heals as we release it and replace it with good attitudes. Dwelling on the past, current offenses, the wicked words or deeds of others causes a fracture in our lives. It unsettles us and makes us suffer. We cannot go back and change it, but we can change our future. As we release our suffering to the Lord as our portion for the day, we can choose to praise Him for His goodness. May goodness and mercy follow you all the days of your life.

Blessing: May the goodness of the Lord chase you down and overcome you with bountiful blessings.

Lord God deliver me from the curses spoken over me. Deliver others from the curses I have spoken over them. Let me bless and not curse Let me speak with words of gentleness, goodness, and kindness. May words go forth and accomplish great things and return unto me. In Jesus Name I pray.

LESSON 16

MEEKNESS/HUMILITY

Humble yourselves before the Lord, and he will lift you up.
James 4:10

Introduction

Meekness is not feeling like you are beneath other people. A synonym is humility. **Humility** is freedom from pride or arrogance.

Lucifer fell from Heaven because he wanted to be like God. (Isaiah 14:13-15) It was his pride that caused him to fall. Lucifer, who became known as Satan, then beguiled Eve with the same temptation to be "like God." She was overcome by pride and lost her humility and trusted in herself. After the fall, God killed an animal for the blood to cover their sins and the skins to clothe them. What were they clothed in before sin? Maybe the glory of God. Maybe the garment of humility. God promised a redeemer to restore them to fellowship with Him.

In the New Testament, Jesus came to earth to redeem what was lost in the fall. He came in the garment of humility. *All of you, clothe yourselves with humility towards one another, because God opposes the proud but gives grace to the humble.1 Peter 5:5*

Garment of Flesh/Pride	Garment of Humility
Garden of Eden	Death of Self-will
Adam and Eve	Pick up your cross
Serpent	Follow Jesus
Pride	Glorify God
Fallen Nature	Returned and Restored

Lesson

Pride is a partition between us and God. **Humility** requires a child-like faith and deep dependency upon God. For this lesson, let us look at the Sermon on the Mount called the Beatitudes in Matthew 5:3-12

1) *"Blessed are the poor in spirit, for theirs is the kingdom of heaven." Matthew 5:3* The key word here is "in spirit", this does not describe our financial situation, but our heart attitude. To be poor in spirit is the opposite of being proud. Only the humble can enter heaven.
2) *Blessed are those who mourn, for they will be comforted. Matthew 5:4* When we mourn for sin, confession is the way to receive comfort. When we mourn for lost souls, it is the grace of God that will comfort us.
3) *Blessed are the meek, for they will inherit the earth.*

Matthew 5:5 Meek is described as gentle, humble, and lowly. It is the meek who choose to allow their trials to bring them to humility, instead of bitterness. They can participate in the work that God has planned for the earth.

4) *Bless are those who hunger and thirst for righteousness, for they will be filled. Matthew 5:6* When we are humble, we recognize our need to be filled of God. Once we are empty of ourselves, we can achieve fullness of God and have complete satisfaction.

5) *Blessed are the merciful, for they will be shown mercy. Matthew 5:7* When we humble ourselves to cooperate with the Holy Spirit in the regeneration process, we will have the mercy that Jesus showed on the cross—we forgive those who wrong us, no matter what! Luke 23:34 says, "Father forgive them for they know not what they do."

6) *Blessed are the pure in heart, for they will see God. Matthew 5:8* A pure heart humbles itself daily before God. It is in this pure state that we can see what God is doing in our lives and in those around us.

7) *Blessed are the peacemakers, for they will be called sons of God. Matthew 5:9* As we humble ourselves and seek peace with God, we can have peace in all our circumstances. When we have peace with God, peace with others follows closely behind.

8) *Blessed are those who are persecuted because of righteousness, for theirs is the kingdom of heaven. Matthew 5:10* As we separate ourselves from the world and draw closer to God, the world will persecute us. It takes a humble person to suffer through persecution without retaliation. 2 Timothy 3:12 says, "... All that will live godly in Christ Jesus shall suffer persecution."

9) *Blessed are you when people insult you, persecute you and falsely say all kinds of evil against you because of me. Matthew 5:11* The true test of humility is when your name is smeared with lies, and you humble yourself enough to trust God with the results.

10) *Rejoice and be glad, because great is your reward in heaven, for in the same way they persecuted the prophets who were before you. Matthew 5:12* When our desire is to please

> God and not ourselves, we will conquer the flesh and walk
> in joy by the power of the Holy Spirit. This involves setting
> our hearts on eternal glory, and not on the temporal things
> around us.

Exercise

On a scale of 1-10 how humble are you?

Application

The true test of humility is humility before God. Luke 16:10 says, "He that is faithful in that which is least, is faithful also in much..." Seek daily to humble yourself in the least of things. Pray to recognize your pride, and put on the garment of humility, as your Christlikeness today.

Principle

Meekness is freedom from arrogance or stubbornness.

Conclusion

Meekness is freedom from anxiety. It is a trusting and faithful walk with the Lord. Freedom from the hinderance of self-consciousness. It is walking with the Lord in gratefulness and not complaining with offenses. May the grumbling of entitlement disappear.

Blessings of humility
• We will inherit the kingdom of heaven.
• We will be comforted.
• We will inherit the earth.
• We will be empty of ourselves and filled with God.
• We will obtain mercy.
• We shall see God.
• We shall be called the children of God.
• Our reward in heaven will be great.

Pride only breeds quarrels, but wisdom is found in those
who take advice. Proverbs 13:10

Dear friend, I bless you to inherit the kingdom of heaven. The kingdom that can live in you now. That you may be comforted, filled with God and able to have the eyes of faith to see him working in your heart. May you be full of mercy. May you be known throughout the land for your great humility. Amen.

LESSON 17

HEALTHY FAITH

But without faith it is impossible to please Him. Hebrews 11:6

Introduction

A fretting and wringing of my hands with a perpetual whine indulging every savage emotion that attempts to take me captive is a good signal that I am not "strong" in faith.

Am I spiritually sick?

Spiritual Sickness
Lukewarm *So, because you are lukewarm—neither hot nor cold—I am about to spit you out of my mouth. Revelations 3:16*
Spiritually asleep – *You hate my instruction and cast my words behind you. Psalm 50:17*
Complacent aka sloth - *As a door turns on its hinges, so a sluggard turns on his bed. Proverbs 26:14*
Spiritually calloused heart – *For this people's heart has become calloused; they hardly hear with their ears, and they have closed their eyes. Otherwise, they might see with their eyes, hear with their ears, understand with their hearts, and turn, and I would heal them. Matthew 13:15*
Spiritually blind – *Leave them; they are blind guides. If the blind lead the blind, both will fall into a pit. Matthew 15:14*

> **Spiritual deaf** – *"...Do you still not understand? Are your <u>hearts hardened</u>? Do you have eyes but fail to see, and ears but fail to hear? And don't you <u>remember</u>?" Mark 8:17b-18a*

Lesson

Faithless

1. **Futile faith** – Without a risen Savior our faith is in vain. *If Christ has not been raised, your faith is futile; you are still in your sins. 1 Corinthians 15:17*

2. **Dead faith** – *You believe that there is one God good! Even the demons believe that—and shudder.* James 2:19 A belief in doctrine without a personal belief in Christ is dead faith.

Levels of Faith

1. **Hardness of Heart = Unbelief** *(11) When they heard that Jesus was alive and that she had seen him, <u>they did not believe it</u>. (12) Afterward Jesus appeared in a different form to two of them while they were walking in the country. (13) These returned and reported it to the rest; but <u>they did not believe them either</u>. (14) Later Jesus appeared to the eleven as they were eating; he rebuked them for their <u>lack of faith</u> and their <u>stubborn refusal</u> (hardness of heart) to believe those who had seen him after he had risen. Mark 16:11-14*

2. **Little Faith-worries a lot.** *If that is how God clothes the grass of the field, which is here today and tomorrow is thrown into the fire, will he not much more clothe you, O you of little faith? Matthew 6:30*

3. **Weak Faith-follows a lot of rules** *Accept him whose faith is weak, without passing judgment on disputable matters. One man's faith allows him to eat everything, but another man, whose faith is weak, eats only vegetables. Romans 14:1-2*

4. **Strong Faith-believing the promises of God** *(19) Without weakening in his faith, he faced the fact that his body was as good as dead—since he was about a hundred years old—and that Sarah's womb was also dead. (20) Yet he did not waver through unbelief regarding the promise of God but was strengthened in his faith and gave glory to God, (21) being fully persuaded that God had power to do what he had promised. Romans 4:19-21*

Maturing in Faith

1. **Contend for the faith** ...*I felt I had to write and urge you to contend for the faith that was once for all entrusted to the saints. Jude 3*

2. **Saving faith** ...*confess with your mouth, "Jesus is Lord," and believe in your heart that God raised him from the dead, you will be saved. Romans 10:9*

3. **Justifying faith** *This righteousness from God comes through faith in Jesus Christ to all who believe. There is no difference, (23) for all have sinned and fall short of the glory of God, (24) and are <u>justified freely by his grace</u> through the redemption that came by Christ Jesus. Romans 3:22-24*

4. **Crucified Self** *I have been crucified with Christ and I no longer live, but Christ lives in me. The life I live in the body, I live by faith in the Son of God, who loved me and gave himself for me. Galatians 2:20*

5. **Righteous faith** ...*The righteous will live by faith. Romans 1:17*

6. **Spiritual Eyes of Faith** *Now faith is being sure of what we hope for and certain of what we do not see. Hebrews 11:1*

7. **Active Faith** *In the same way, faith by itself, if it is not accompanied by action, is dead. James 2:17*

8. **Mature Faith** *You see that a person is justified by what he does and not by faith alone. James 2:24*

Exercise

Determine your level of faith and start intentionally growing in faith.

Application

Three Commands to Develop my Faith

Come, Learn, and Find

If my burdens seem too heavy to bear, I may need to come to Jesus and give the burdens to Him.

Come to me, all you who are weary and burdened, and I will give you rest. Take my yoke upon you and learn from me, for I am gentle and humble in heart, and you will find rest for your souls. For my yoke is easy and my burden is light. Matthew 11:28-30

Follow me

It is my responsibility to follow Christ by giving him my whole heart, soul and mind. (Mark 12:30)

Then said Jesus to his disciples, *"If anyone would come after me, he must deny himself and take up his cross and follow me. Matthew 16:24*

Abide "in" me

Abide in me, and I in you. As the branch cannot bear fruit of itself, except it abide in the vine; no more can you, except you abide in me. John 15:4

It is in this close abiding relationship with Christ that we find the "rest" for our souls we so desperately crave. This abiding fellowship takes the focus off me, myself and I and any other problem that is distracting me and places my focus on Christ and his enduring love. Then I find courage and strength to face all the giants.

Nay, in all these things we are more than conquerors through him that loved us. Romans 8:37

Principle

We cannot please God without faith.

Conclusion

And without faith it is impossible to please God, because anyone who comes to him must believe that he exists and that he rewards those who earnestly seek him. Hebrews 11:6 Salvation starts with a step of faith. As we see in Scripture, salvation is a gift and cannot be earned. *... for it is by grace we have been saved, through faith—and this not from ourselves, it is the gift of God— (10) For we are God's workmanship, created in Christ Jesus to do good works, which God prepared in advance for us to do. Ephesians 8:8,10* The works we do will reveal the depth of our relationship with the Lord. *...Let your light shine before men, that they may see your good deeds and praise your Father in heaven. Matthew 5:16*

Now let us evaluate our growth in faith:

Feeble Faith
1) Prayerlessness
2) No desire to read the Word
3) Do not think the Word applies today
4) Think like a Deist (God put us here and walked away.)
5) No vision for the future
6) Eyes on temporal things
7) Little faith (fainthearted–gives up easily)
8) Confusion
9) Depression
10) Dysfunctional coping skills: caffeine, food, pills, alcohol, drugs, etc.

STRONG Faith
1) Disciplined prayer life
2) Watchful and waiting
3) Hungering and thirsting for God's Word
4) Longing for deeper fellowship with Christ
5) Saturating self with the Word
6) Growing & maturing in faith
7) Purposeful to develop the Fruit of the Spirit
8) Accountable to others for good character
9) Humbling self
10) Serving God and being used by the Lord
11) Steadfast maturity
12) Wrestling unbelief and making no provisions for the flesh

Nay, in all the things we are more than conquerors through him that loved us. Romans 8:3

My Lord and my God redeem what was stolen and restore what was lost. Be my refuge and my strength. A very present help in times of trouble. Help me to choose to be still and know that you are my God and a mighty fortress in every storm. Psalm 46:1,10

LESSON 18

SELF-CONTROL

*People will be lovers of themselves, lovers of money, boastful, proud, abusive, disobedient to their parents, ungrateful, unholy, without love, unforgiving, slanderous, **without self-control**, brutal, not lovers of the good, treacherous, rash, conceited, lovers of pleasure rather than lovers of God—having a form of godliness but denying its powers. Have nothing to do with them. 2 Timothy 3:3*

Introduction

Self-control is the power to say NO to yourself. It is the power to discipline your thoughts, speech and actions to think or do as you instruct yourself to do. It is an inward strength, courage, and moral restraint to **master yourself**. Proverbs talks about "owning" my own spirit. To own myself, I must have a strong fortified will to wall off anything that would be an enemy to my soul. *He that has no rule over his own spirit is like a city that is broken down, and without walls (or who lack self-control NIV). Proverbs 25:28KJV* There are two other words in the Bible that mean self-control: temperance and sober.

Lesson

Refuting Lies
1. **Am I ever in charge of how deep I go into sin?** *Do you not know that when you offer yourselves to someone to obey him as slaves, you are slaves to the one whom you obey—whether you are slaves to sin, which leads to death, or to obedience which leads to righteousness. Romans 6:16*
2. **No one tells me what to do!** *There is a way which seems right unto a man, but the end thereof are the ways of death. Proverbs 14:12; 16:25*
3. **Can't I just sow my wild oats?** *Death and Destruction are never satisfied, and neither are the eyes of men. Proverbs 27:20*

Finding Freedom

1. **What do I need to master myself?** Paul says, *"(25) Everyone who competes in the games goes into <u>strict training</u>. They do it to get a crown that will not last; but we do it to get a crown that will last forever. (26) Therefore, I do not fight like a man beating the air, (27) No, I <u>beat my body and make it my slave</u> so that after I have preached to others, I myself will not be <u>disqualified for the prize</u>." 1 Corinthians 9:25-27*

2. **How do I find freedom from my flesh?** *You have been set free and have <u>become slaves to righteousness.</u> Romans 6:18* You can become a slave to righteousness, by just doing what is right.

3. **How do I live in freedom?** *For if you live according to the sinful nature, you will die; but if by the Spirit you <u>put to death the misdeeds of the body</u>, you will live. Romans 8:13*

4. **How can I put the death the misdeeds of the body?** *Because those who are led by the Spirit are the sons of God. For you did not receive a spirit that makes you a <u>slave again to fear</u>, but you received the Spirit of sonship. And by him <u>we cry, "Abba, Father,"</u> ... Romans 8:14-15*

5. **How do I escape temptation?** *God is faithful; he will not let you be tempted beyond what you can bear. But when you are tempted, he will also provide you a way out so that you can stand up under it. 1 Corinthians 10:13*

6. **Can I return to places of temptation?** *But put on the Lord Jesus Christ, and make not provisions for the flesh, to fulfil the lusts thereof. Romans 13:14KJV*

7. **What if I do not have enough self-control to make right choices?** *If you then, though you are evil, know how to give good gifts to your children, how much more will* <u>*your Father in heaven give the Holy Spirit*</u> *to those who* ***ask him****!" Luke 11:13* ASK FOR HELP!

What is the promise? *Blessed is the man who perseveres under trial (temptation), because when he has stood the test, he will receive the* ***crown of life*** *that God has promised to those who love him. James 1:12*

Exercise

Name what area in your life needs the most self-control.

Application

Without listening for instructions and yielding ourselves to our authorities we have little protection from the enemy devouring our lives with fleshly self-indulgences. **Instructions:** *(8) Be* ***self-controlled and alert*** *Your enemy the devil prowls around like a roaring lion looking for someone to devour. (9)* ***Resist*** *him,* ***standing firm*** *in the faith... 1 Peter 5:8-9*

Set up little disciplines in your life and practice self-control in the smaller things and then when the bigger choices arise, you will be stronger to say NO to yourself. *Whoever can be trusted with very little can also be trusted with much, and whoever is dishonest with very little will also be dishonest with much. Luke 16:10*

Principle

True freedom is freedom not to sin.

Conclusion

Behaviors are driven by what is in front of us. Use self-control to determine what you place in front of your eyes; what you listen to and where you go. Take control of your life by walking in the Spirit and exercising your sonship to enjoy fruit of the Spirit: love, joy, peace, patience, kindness, goodness, faithfulness, gentleness, and **self-control**. Galatians 5:22-23

Finally, "(13) <u>prepare your minds</u> for action; <u>be self-controlled</u>; <u>set your hope</u> fully on the grace to be given you when Jesus Christ is revealed. (14) As obedient children **do not conform** to the evil desires you had when you lived in ignorance. (16) ... for it is written: 'Be holy, because I am holy.'" 1 Peter 1:13-14,16

Lord, help us to master our own selves. Give us dominion over our own souls. May we choose what to think, what to say and what to do by the power and the authority of our loving God Amen.

Diving Deeper

What are the commands in Joshua 1:7-9?

1) Be strong and courageous. (Repeated 3 times.)
2) Be careful to obey.
3) Do not turn to the right or to the left.
4) Do not let this book depart from your mouth.
5) Meditate in the Word of God-day and night.
6) Be careful to do everything in it.
7) Do not be afraid.
8) Do not be discouraged.

What are the promises?

1) You will be prosperous and successful.
2) The Lord will go with you wherever you go.

Why is this necessary for Joshua to be strong and courage and meditate in God's Word? *Joshua will lead the people to inherit the land.

Who are you leading?
Where are you leading them?
What are you meditating or thinking on?

Lord Jesus, help us to focus. Help us to meditate on truth and release our sorrows. Help us to correct our self by focusing on thoughts that are stronger than our circumstances. Keep us in perfect peace as we keep our minds steadfast, trusting you. Isaiah 26:3

Praying Scriptures

Lay your problems, sorrows, regrets on the altar of God. Ask Him to send you peace. Turn these Scriptures into prayer.

1) In you, O LORD, I have taken refuge; let me never be put to shame (confusion). Psalm 71:1

Prayer:
O God stop the confusion. Please, give me refuge in You. Help me to make good decisions. Amen

2) Cast all your anxiety on Him because He cares for you. 1 Peter 5:7

Prayer:
O God, I give you this problem (name it). I am grieving and sad about (name it). I regret (name it).

3) Yeh though I walk through the valley of the shadow of death, I will fear no evil, for you are with me; your rod and your staff, they comfort me. Surely goodness and love (mercy) will follow me all the days of my life. Psalm 23:4

Prayer:
O God protect me from death and take away all my fears. Lord, be my shepherd and comfort me. Let Your goodness and mercy follow me all the days of my life. Amen

Praying Scripture is the quickest and most powerful path to peace.

Habits for Success

1. Respect Authority
2. Protect your Good Name
3. Learn to Stand Alone
4. Guard the Truth
5. Take Responsibility for your Actions
6. Be Honorable and fair in your Decisions
7. Make Morally Good Decisions
8. Live with Self-control and Moderation with all things that are moral, legal, and acceptable
9. Give a Good Days Work without Complaint
10. Guard all Entrusted to your Hands

Let Steel Form in your Soul

1. Abandon the selfish side of self
2. Ask God only for His perfect will
3. Obey completely even if it costs you
4. Complete trust and faith in God for deliverance in famine, afflictions, persecutions, trials, tribulations, addictions and even in death

Devotions

Devotions are rich times of fellowship with God. They are times we can come to God with a question and receive insight, direction and peace for the day. This settling our self at the feet of Jesus is the thing that is most necessary.

As Jesus and his disciples were on their way, he came to a village where a woman named Martha opened her home to him. She had a sister called Mary, who sat at the Lord's feet listening to what he said. But Martha was distracted by all the preparations that had to be made. She came to him and asked, "Lord, don't you care that my sister has left me to do the work by myself? Tell her to help!" "Martha, Martha, the Lord, answered, "you are worried and upset about many things, but only one thing is needed. Mary has chosen what is better, and it will not be takes away from her." Luke 10:38-42

How do I stop anxiety in its tracts?

- I believe it is this settling our self at the feet of Jesus that stops the hurrying and distractions.

- It is our lack of understanding of who I am in Christ and the work of salvation He is doing in me that keeps me trapped in anxiety.
  - Perhaps I do not understand how to use the blessed resources available to me.
  - Perhaps I have never been taught how to trust Christ in every area of my life.
  - Perhaps I never knew peace abides only in a trusting relationship with my Lord.
  - Perhaps I have not understood how to go into my prayer closet (inner heart chamber) and shut the door.
- So could the root cause of my anxiety be prayerlessness. Oh, how quickly I can stray.

The command is to "pray without ceasing." 1 Thessalonians 5:17

We breathe without ceasing. Could it be that our prayer should be spontaneous and so much a part of our life that it mimics breathing?

Prayer is work.

It is a moment-by-moment awareness of the presence of the Holy Spirit living within us to be our teacher and our helper. (John 14:26) Jesus says He is praying for the Comforter to abide in us forever. John 14:16

How do I abide in Christ and not in anxiety?

The key is to "abide" (dwell) in Christ (John 15), in a moment-by-moment quiet reflection of the truths of God's Word within my Spirit. This is not possible unless I am feeding my Spirit the Living Word throughout the day.

My anxiety is a STOP sign to call me back to the Lord and to His Word and to a rehearsing of His promises within my heart. This abiding fellowship is rich and pleasant. Abiding in Christ is a solid foundation to weather any anxious storm.

Next time anxiety comes, ask yourself, "Where am I abiding?"

What would cause me to wander in paranoia and reject love?

Could it be unbelief? Do we really believe God loves us and wants intimate fellowship with us? Today, say to yourself a dozen times, "I am loved." When I first did this, it made me weep. I know I am loved, but I did not hold sacred the love God gave me from Himself or others.

Possibly a wounded heart cannot hold love. I rejected God's love and His accompanying peace and chose to walk in anxiety.

This anxiety became such a familiar companion that I thought the anxiety was me!

This lie set up a stronghold and I was BOUND in CHAINS.

While daily walking in anxiety, I forgot the power that lives within me.

I forgot I could stir up the Holy Spirit through prayer and fasting and find the Prince of Prince. (Matthew 17:20;Isaiah 9:6)

A Storm Inside of Me

It is this storm that drives me to dysfunctional coping skills. Quiet the storm and stop the addiction.

Sometimes the storm inside of me rages so violently that I experience waves of terror and am left emotionally distraught and physically drained.

One time in particular:

My stomach was churning. My anxiety high. I was snippy and agitated. My mind was full of racing thoughts. Fear of the future was overwhelming me.

And then... I cried out, "Oh God, if you can calm the wind and the waves of a great sea, surely you can calm this storm in me."

Immediately, it was as if Jesus was awakened and heard my cry. There was peace in my heart and complete and indescribable calm that came over me. Jesus spoke "Quiet! Be still!" to my heart.

Quiet! Be still!

Mark 4:35-41 That day when evening came, he said to his disciples, "Let us go over to the other side."

If Jesus has said we are going to the other side, trust that he will make a way.

Leaving the crowd behind, they took him along, just as he was, in the boat...A furious squall came up, and the waves broke over the boat, so that it was nearly swamped. Jesus was in the stern, sleeping on a cushion.

The disciples woke him and said to him, "Teacher, don't you care if we drown?"

Of course, Jesus cares if you are drowning! Cry out to him.

He got up, rebuked the wind and said to the waves, "Quiet! Be still!" Then the wind died down and it was completely calm.

Ask Jesus to speak to your storm.

He said to his disciples, "Why are you so afraid? Do you still have no faith?"

Could our problem be lack of faith? Do we need to learn to cry out to Jesus to save us when we are drowning?

They were terrified and asked each other, "Who is this? Even the wind and the waves obey him!"

So have courage and faith! We serve a mighty God!

Choose Sides in this Battle!

I felt my prayers were scattered and feeble and would hide myself from God.

Anxiety shrouded me in DARKNESS and robbed me of my relationship with a loving God.

But the "peace of God" is mine. Promised to me. Why do I not know this peace?

Could it be that I have laid down my greatest weapon?

Could it be my weapon was stolen by circumstances?

Could my flesh have convinced me of the vanity of prayer?

Has the noise in my head and distractions become obstacles between me and my Lord?

O friend of God, elevating this emotion of anxiety places you on the wrong side!!!

Anxiety is on the side of the enemy!

Now refuse anxiety!

Rise up and claim what is yours!

Pray and seek God's face with a fierceness of the warrior you were created to be.

Claim your helmet, belt, breastplate, shield, shoes, and especially your sword. Ephesians 6:10-20

Claim the "peace of God that surpasses all understanding." Philippians 4:6-7 *"Do not be anxious about anything, but in everything, by prayer and petition, with thanksgiving, present your requests to God. And the peace of God, which transcends all understanding, will guard your hearts and your minds in Christ Jesus."*

When this amazing peace comes you will know you have empowered yourself through faith to conquer your unbelief and are now on the right side of the battle.

Fear of the Future

If your bent is to always be anxious with knots in your stomach and your muscles aching from the tension, you are in good company. I too am prone to anxiousness if I am not intentionally fighting it. It took years to recognize I could take dominion over my thought life. Here are some pointers:

1) Do not meditate on things outside your power to change. Detach and let them go.

2) Cry out to God to give you GRACE to trust Him more.

3) When I did this, the Lord brought a verse to my mind: "Though He slay me, yet I will trust in Him." (Job 13:15KJV)

My fears were immediately calmed, my situation was immediately measured against the glory of eternity. Then I gladly received this test to trust God and chose in my heart to place my faith in Christ. I chose to use the situation as hallowed ground It then became a place of eternal weight in glory. (2 Corinthians 4:17)

Instructions on How to Develop Spiritual Eyes

For our light and momentary troubles are achieving for us an eternal glory that far outweighs them all. So, we fix our eyes not on what is seen, but on what is unseen. For what is seen is temporary, but what is unseen is eternal." 2 Corinthians 4:17-18

Fix your eyes on the author of peace. 1 Corinthians 14:33

Accountability Questions (2 Peter 1:10)

1. Have you developed a love for Scripture and Prayer and spend time focusing on the Word daily?

2. Is there anything you are thinking or doing that is not glorifying to God?

3. Are you harboring any anger or bitterness?

4. Is there anyone you need to forgive or anyone you need to ask forgiveness from?

5. Have you elevated anxiety above faith?

6. Have you been able to control your thoughts and your tongue today?

7. Have you been hiding or lying about anything?

8. Can you be trusted to be kind and patient in your relationships?

9. Can you be patient with yourself and extent grace to yourself during times of stress?

10. Have you learned to do your best and wait on God to work out the rest?

Next, I need to be on a quest to find safe friends and healthy support. Right now, I can be responsible for my own self, my own thoughts, feelings and behaviors.

Scripture   **Prayer**

Shift your Focus

Sunday

Monday

Tuesday

Wednesday

Thursday

Friday

Saturday

Practical Tips

Have I:
1) Made my bed?
2) Taken out my trash?
3) Cleaned up my yard?
4) Wash, dry, iron and put away my laundry?
5) Clean my car?
If I cannot manage my own life, what is prohibiting me from doing so?

What do I need to change in my life to give me the ability to have peace?

If I mind my own business, I can have the energy to care for myself and address my character flaws and position myself with others who can mentor, encourage, and hold me accountable for my actions.

Reflective Thinking

A clear conscience brings a good night sleep.

- How can I practice quiet reflective thinking? Can I set a time of day or a special place to meditate and reflect on my day?

- Do I understand that often I cannot think my way through a problem, no matter how hard or how long I think about it? This is obsessive thinking, not quiet and productive thinking. Can you tell the difference?

- Do I know how to meditate on wholesome thoughts?

- What can I do to quiet my fears?

- Do I know how to stay in the present moment and enjoy my day?

- Do I know how to detach from toxic people and circumstances I cannot control? This skill produces great peace.

- What consumes my passive thinking? Passive thinking are uninvited thoughts that take over quickly.

- How can I mature and develop a quiet mind?

- Do I know how to refuse a negative thought and replace it with a positive one?

- Do I recognize a toxic person who controls my thinking or emotions?

- What problems (from other people) would I need to release to find peace?

- What self-care priorities do I have in my daily routine?

- Do I need to say NO to others to better manage my time and prevent me from being overwhelmed?

- How could I tactfully set boundaries with others who dominate my time?

- Is there a circumstance that has me paralyzed to make decisions?

- Can I be manipulated with urgency and factitious deadlines to make quick and foolish decisions?

- How do my loved ones extort from me financially? Do they use other authorities to manipulate me? (The landlord, attorney, fees and fines must be paid *now*.) This is commonly done on the day before you receive your paycheck. Watch for this cycle. Some squander their money and use your money for monthly expenses. Step back and let them learn.

- How can I prepare to change? Can I be slow to make decisions and involve other responsible people?

- Who do I have in my life that would protect me from an abuser or manipulative person?

- What would I need to do to be compassionate and gracious to myself?

- Are there expectations I need to detach from? Are they mine or someone else's?

Negative Emotional Triggers

- Which negative emotion(s) controls me?

  - Anger
  - Bitterness
  - Fear
  - Worry and Anxiety
  - Depression

If I am not an angry person, but compassionate and empathetic, it is necessary for me to use controlled anger to protect myself. Allowing myself to indulge some angry feelings can help me build a wall of protection around my heart to safeguard me from irresponsible adults. If I am an angry person, I need to dig beneath the anger to find my emotional wounds and fears.

Permission

1) I give you permission to say no.
2) I give you permission to walk away from someone who only makes temporary changes to fool themselves and others.
3) I give you permission to grieve and not be responsible for a person who refuses to correct themselves or allow others to hold them accountable.
4) I give you permission to give others back their own problems. This is the loving thing to do for them and yourself.

Unmet Needs

When I have unmet needs, what negative behaviors do I exhibit?

- Mind altering substances (even prescription medications)
- Alcohol, excessive sugar, or overeating
- Sexually acting out
- Suicidal/homicidal/angry/bitter/self-pity/grieving rumination
- Compulsive shopping or gambling, television, etc.
- **Passive/Aggressive Behaviors**

What are my unmet needs?

- Can I ask for what I need from safe people?
- Do I know how to reach out to others?
- Can I take care of my needs first? Givers and empaths do not normally care for themselves.
- Do I have a safe support group or close friends who understand?
- If there is no one safe in my life, can I be safe for myself?

Obsessive Thinking Traps

- **Fantasy thinking**
  - I compulsively escape the circumstances and reactions of others with fairytale daydreaming.
- **Trauma thinking**
  - I spontaneously and anxiously role play future devastation: bankruptcy, abandonment, kidnapping, homelessness, prison, and funerals.
- **Automatic replay thinking**
  - I persistently replay a traumatic event, hurtful gesture, or unkind word.
  - One harsh criticism gives me an avalanche of past wounds to rehearse. (This means I have not dealt with past trauma.)
  - I become paralyzed with self-pity type of behaviors. This can quickly overwhelm me with depression and isolation. It can be exhibited by overeating, staying in bed or addictive behavior patterns.

Boundaries with my Passive Thinking

Goals for my thinking:

1. Self-controlled
2. Healthy
3. Honorable
4. Faithful
5. Kind
6. Patient
7. Accepting
8. Releasing
9. True
10. Hopeful

When you hear thoughts that are robbing you of the enjoyment of your day, reject them and purposefully think wholesome thoughts. Give yourself ten minutes once or twice a day to think about problems and possible solutions. Set a timer. Keep a running list, spend those ten minutes worrying, fretting or being angry. When the timer goes off and you have found no viable solutions, get up and enjoy your day.

Forgiveness

if we don't forgive, it is hard to find forgiveness.

- Forgiveness should not allow someone else access to abuse us again.
- Forgiveness is free.
- Trust is earned.

If we indulge in a lack of forgiveness, it will:

- Robs us of our happiness.
- Contaminate our thinking
- Contaminate our speech
- Cause troubles in our other relationships

How do I forgive

How do I forgive? Even, if I do not feel like it?
Forgiveness is a choice and the right thing to do.
Forgiveness does not pardon the offender from consequences.
Forgiveness is for my benefit.
Forgiveness is not forgetfulness. It needs a strong boundary until trust is earned.

Some things are unforgiveable. But the person or the event cannot have power over your daily life. Move it to a shelf in your mind. Stuff it in the freezer and don't feel it every day until you are ready to finish the work of grieving, anger, bitter, etc.... and let it go.

Bitterness

Lack of forgiveness will end in bitterness that will ooze a little at a time or explode in exaggeration over trivial matters. If you leech bitter poison onto waitresses or retail workers, become cognizant of the unsafe person in your life you are not safe to confront. Journal or find a trusted friend and unload the pain in a healthy manner. This will help you detach your heart from an unsafe person who may never acknowledge their wrong or ask for forgiveness.

- Bitterness robs our joy for today.
- Bitterness clouds our memories of yesterday.
- Bitterness overshadows every future relationship with lonely walls of self-protection.

Forgiveness

- If we do not forgive, we will be the one who is tormented.
- Un-forgiveness holds us hostage in hatred, anger, and suffering.
- Forgiveness does not mean forgetfulness.
- Forgiveness should not open us up to an unsafe relationship.
- If we accept the suffering caused by another and forgive our offender this releases us.
    - Forgiveness brings us emotional stability and tranquility.
    - Forgiveness softens our hearts to become responsible for our part of the problem.
    - Forgiveness forges the way for others to humbly repent.
    - Repentance is a fresh, clean slate.
    - Repentance is permission to move forward, learn, grow and **not repeat the past.**
    - **Forgiveness is separate from reconciliation.**

Reconciliation

- Reconciliation comes when the other person acknowledges their dysfunctional behaviors and develops a plan to change with structured accountability.
- Reconciliation, if pursued too quickly, may cause your loved one to fall back into old habits of dominance and manipulation. It may also allow you to be abused again.

Repentance

Repentance for our dysfunctional behaviors is part of our growth process.

Repentance reminds us that codependency is sick love and is not helping others find maturity, stability, or independence.

Repentance for abusive behaviors covers and releases us to live a life free from shame, guilt, and self-condemnation.

Healing and Deliverance Verses

1) **Fear not** for I am with you be not dismayed, for I am your God. I will **strengthen you** and help you. I will **uphold you** with my right hand of my righteousness. Isaiah 41:10

2) But He was wounded for our transgressions, He was bruised for our iniquities: the chastisement of our peace was upon Him; and **with His stripes we are healed**. Isaiah 53:5

3) The Lord is near them that are of a **broken heart**; and saves such as be of a **contrite spirit. Psalm 34:18**

4) Bless the Lord, O my soul, and all that is within me, bless His holy name. Bless the Lord, O my soul, and forget not all his benefits: Who **forgives all** my iniquities, who **heals all** my diseases. Who **redeems my life** from destruction, who **crowns me** with loving-kindness and tender mercies. Who satisfies my mouth with good things; so that my youth is renewed like the eagle's. Psalm 103:1-5

5) Is any among you afflicted? **Let him pray...** Is any sick among you? Let him call for the elders of the church; and **let them pray over him**, anointing him with oil in the name of the Lord.; And the prayer of faith shall save the sick, and the Lord shall raise him up; and if he has committed sins, **they shall be forgiven.** Confess your faults one to another, and **pray for each other**, that you may be healed. James 5:13-16

6) **Have mercy on me,** O Lord; for I am weak. **O Lord, heal me**; for my bones are vexed.

7) Return, O Lord, **deliver my soul;** oh, **save me** for your mercies' sake. Psalm 6:2,4

8) I said unto the Lord, **be merciful unto me: heal my soul**; for I have sinned against you. Psalm 41:4

9) He heals the broken in heart, He **binds up our wounds.** Psalm 147:3

10) He sent His Word, and **healed them**, and **delivered them** from their destructions. Psalm 107:20

11) **Trust in the Lord with all my heart**; and lean not unto my own understanding. In all my ways acknowledge Him, and He shall direct my paths. Be not wise in thine own eyes: fear the Lord and depart from evil. Proverbs 3:5-6

12) **Pleasant words** are as a honeycomb, sweet to the soul, and health to the bones. Proverbs 16:24

13) A **merry heart** does good like a medicine: but a broken spirit dries up the bones. Proverbs 17:22

14) Peace I leave with you, my **peace I give unto you**: not as the world gives, give I unto you. **Let not your heart be troubled, neither let it be afraid.** John 14:27

Conclusion

For God did not give us a spirit of timidity (fear), but a spirit of power, of love and of self-discipline (sound mind). 2 Timothy 1:7 Could this mean that a sound mind comes from self-discipline?

Journal Prompts

Journal to explore, release and change negative emotions. I journal beside a shredder. This way I am free to release all exaggerated emotions safely. If I keep the journal pages for a few days, I can reread them and laugh at how irrational I can be at times of stress. Writing forty ranting pages of what I cannot control brings out thoughts, emotions and lies I did not know I believed. I journal until I can release the problem and unscramble my thinking and find peace. I start journaling with I hate...I am angry about... I am hurt about... I am disappointed about... I end my journaling with I forgive, I release, I am grateful for...

- How much time do I spend in negative rumination each day? Journal your negative thoughts, then attempt to change them to a positive thought. For example: I cannot do anything right. Now change this to a positive statement. I can be patient with myself and do the best that I can do.

- Is my sleep interrupted by my worries? If so, lie upon the bed at night and visually put all worries in a box and push them away. Then breathe deeply and clear your mind and focus on relaxing every part of your body. Start at your feet and work your way up. Let your breathing begin to deepen and lengthen.

- How much do I suffer for other people's immature decisions? Identify and write out all the things that are causing you suffering. Now detach from this suffering by seeing the problem outside of you. It is not you, nor does it need to be inside of you. Move the emotional suffering to a safe distance from you. You may find your physical pain is associated with your emotional suffering, you will have energy to work a plan to develop strong boundaries, regain your physical, mental and emotional stamina.

- What if my suffering is from the divorce, loss of a child, death or imprisonment of a loved one? Grieve and detach from the loss of a dream or the sorrow of losing a loved one, then you can reshape your love for the person in a more realistic manner. If our loved one has died, we can comfort ourselves with memories of what we loved about them; and release any memory that causes suffering. We can reach out to a grief recovery group.

- Can I mature and allow others to experience their own suffering? As maturing adults, we do not want to rescue others from consequences, but we can have compassion and comfort them in their suffering. We can also guide them to let their suffering bring about lasting change in their lives for the better.

- Can I feel compassion without being responsible to act? If I relapse back into being over responsible when others are suffering, I can reach out to supportive strong friends for balance.

- Can I find grace if I am suffering with toxic emotions? If I relapse into emotional immaturity, I can reach out to others to comfort me.

SMALL GROUP RULES

1) Give everyone an opportunity to speak.
2) Keep the discussion to the topic.
3) We are not here to "fix" each other. We are here to support and encourage one another.
4) If you do not want to share, simply say "pass" when it comes to your turn.
5) It is vital that this is a safe place for everyone. No negative, judgmental, or condemning comments. The Rule is LOVE!
6) Confidentiality is mandatory and is taken very seriously.
7) Whatever is spoken in this room, stays in this room.
8) If during the week, you discuss another member's comments among one another, it is to be in the spirit of prayer and encouragement and not in mockery or ridicule. No gossiping or slandering will be tolerated.
9) There will be a release of anyone who wants to leave after the lesson and discussion time.
10) There will often be added extra time of sharing at the end of the group for those with heavy burdens who want to share their struggles and receive individual prayer or for those who want to stay and encourage those struggling.

LEADERSHIP GUIDELINES

Dishonorable Leadership	Honorable Leadership
Anger	Happy Countenance
Use of fear tactics	Approachable
Threats/Bullying	Patient and Kind
Retaliation for being confronted	Gracious; holds others accountable
Hasty/Rash	Treats everyone the same
Impatient	Good self-identity
Arrogant	Good boundaries
Values self, money or project goals more than others	Good mentors Good relationships
Holds a grudge	Unemotional decision maker
Plays favorites	Leads through serving
Casts confusion on situations to blame shift	Humble- Leads with power and under submission to their authority
Makes emotional decisions not principally based decisions	Will do what is right, no matter the consequences
Denies problems	Good listener
Deals only with superficial problems	Forgives easily; coaches weaker ones; encourages others.
Ignores the main problem	Identifies root problems
Does not seek counsel	Seek many counselors
Ask impossible things	Able to plan and develop goals
Unrealistic/Demanding	Able to follow through with a plan
*Adapted from observation of the behaviors of Daniel and Nebuchadnezzar the pagan king in the book of Daniel.	Always same level of emotional availability

Rules: No bullying or verbal abuse ever!
Kind, patient but sometimes very firm!

GOOD FOLLOWER

1. Respects Authority
2. Protects Good Name
3. Learns to Stand Alone (not follow a crowd)
4. Guards the truth
5. Takes responsibility for actions
6. Honorable and fair in decisions
7. Makes good sound financial decisions
8. Lives with Self-Control
9. Moderation in all things
10. Gives good days work without complaint
11. Always on time; dependable
12. Never gossips, slanders, or accuses
13. Takes any issues up the ladder through the chain of command
14. Guards all that is entrusted into their hands; trustworthy
15. Refuses to do anything illegal, unethical, or immoral

*You must learn to be a good follower to be a good leader.

AUTHOR'S BIOGRAPHIES

Angie G. Meadows graduated from St Mary's School of Nursing as a Registered Nurse, Marshall University with a bachelor's in nursing and Ohio State University with a master's in nursing. Angie has been a keen observer of human behaviors and has coached many enablers along with those with anxiety, depression, domestic violence, trauma, and substance use disorders to heal, mature emotionally and recover their lives. She often volunteers to teach teenager and youth on Developmental Emotional Maturity Skills. She is currently a mother, grandmother, speaker, and writer. Angie hosts a podcast called Rock of Recovery. Angie's favorite pastime is quilting and disciplining others. Recently, she has become an ordained minister.